Secret Scars

Secret Scars

One woman's story of overcoming self-harm

Abigail Robson

Authentic

LONDON ● ATLANTA ● HYDERABAD

First published 2007 by Authentic Media
9 Holdom Avenue, Bletchley, Milton Keynes, Bucks, MK1 1QR, UK
285 Lynnwood Avenue, Tyrone, GA 30290, USA
OM Authentic Media
Medchal Road, Jeedimetla Village, Secunderabad 500 055, A.P., India
www.authenticmedia.co.uk
Authentic Media is a division of Send the Light Ltd., a company limited by
guarantee (registered charity no. 270162)

British Library Cataloguing in Publication Data
A catalogue record for this book is available from the
British Library

ISBN 978-1-85078-721-1

Cover Design by Rachel Myatt
Print Management by Adare Carwin
Printed and bound by J.H. Haynes & Co., Sparkford

For Anne, who told me I should write,
And for my mum, who told me I could

Foreword

I have written, spoken and counselled on the subject of eating disorders for many years, and one of my greatest joys is to hear from people who are living in freedom from their eating disorders. As do many of the letters that come across my desk, Abbie's letter to me hesitantly began, "I don't know if you remember me but . . ." While it's true that I don't remember everyone, I remember Abbie very well indeed.

I can still see myself sitting cross-legged with Abbie on the conference room floor at the end of one of our residential weeks, as we talked through her "going-home plan." I was fully aware of her self-hatred and vulnerability and, as I walked away, I remember praying, "Lord, let her make it!" She'd received a revelation of self-worth during the week and I knew that the only One who could sustain her through the journey she faced as she contemplated letting go of the need to indulge in cold showers and self-harm was Jesus.

Abbie's book is a testimony to the goodness of God and to her desire to follow him. Through honestly relating her own journey, she opens the door for those with similar issues to have a voice. She is empowering the powerless. *Secret Scars* offers revelation and insight concerning the mindset and behavior of self-harmers to friends and carers who often lack adequate understanding of these complex issues. Abbie brings out into the open the way children and teenagers think and form concepts and beliefs. She exposes the subtle strongholds of fantasy, lies and deception. She reveals the power of personality, perfection and sensitivity in the development of mental illness. And she shows the impact that loss of identity has in mirroring the behavioral patterns of others, and hence the necessity for a concrete understanding of identity in Christ.

Those who have suffered or are suffering from self-harm, eating disorders, perfection and/or identity struggles will relate to the battles fought and won within these pages; and those who "stand alongside" will have their eyes opened to the inner world of sufferers. My prayer is that through reading Abbie's story you may be transformed. I count it a privilege to have been one link in the recovery chain for Abbie, and I enjoy her working alongside me in helping those who are still trapped. I'm proud of you, Abbie.

Helena Wilkinson
Gower, Swansea
February 2006

A note to readers . . .

Although this book is autobiographical, I have changed many names and identifying characteristics to protect the privacy of those who are part of my story. Some characters are also amalgamations of different people. I have made these alterations in order to preserve the anonymity of those who, for various reasons, prefer to remain so, while also preserving the integrity of the story. Thank you for understanding this.

1

Once, in a desperate attempt to stop myself from splintering my shinbone with a hammer, I phoned an old friend to tell her that I didn't know how long I could keep up the charade.

I was alone at home, which was never a good idea. It was a Thursday, and I had a day off work. It began just like all my other days off. I finally threw off my quilt much later than I'd intended, rebuking myself for my laziness, but not really sure what to do. I wandered around from room to room, achieving nothing.

Eventually, I decided that housework was the way to go. I vacuumed every inch of the floor and scrubbed the old olive green bathroom until it should have shone – although I knew it never would. Such vigorous cleaning made me feel like I'd achieved something, and I decided that I had burned off enough calories to allow myself lunch. So I fixed myself a crisp bread and cottage cheese, with a garnish of paper-thin cucumber slices.

But food was a luxury I didn't deserve. I heard the voices in my head, sneering at me. "What makes you think you're entitled to lunch? You're worthless! You should feel guilty for even considering eating!" I couldn't stand it any more. I only knew one way to make it stop.

I retrieved a razor blade from my secret stash in a box under the bed and scored lines across my arms. Tiny globules of blood welled up, and then joined together into one thick red line. As I watched the blood drip onto the strategically-placed toilet paper, I felt calmer, hardly noticing the stinging pain. I spread the blood with the tip of my finger, drawing scarlet patterns on my skin, relishing every tiny sensation. Cutting turned the tide, and just one swish of a blade washed quiet over chaos.

With my roommate out at work, I could do whatever I wanted without worrying about him finding out my secret. I could take my time getting the panic back under control. Strange as it may seem, panic was actually an excuse for me to indulge in self-harm. My addiction to cutting myself with razorblades had taken over my life. I hated my body, but at the same time I had a morbid fascination with what lay just out of sight. What did my body look like on the inside? How far could I push the barriers of skin and pain?

My head reverberated with condemning barbs tumbling over each other. I heard it all but I couldn't hear anything clearly. It was all too much and cutting was the only way to get some peace and quiet.

Once I'd hidden away my blades, patched up my arm with gauze, and put my blood-stained clothes in the washing machine, I wandered. I felt dazed and light-headed. The voices were muffled now, but they were still there. "Is this what it feels like to be on drugs? Maybe I should try drugs," I thought. But then, suddenly, a better idea popped into my head.

I could hit my shinbone with a hammer.

"No way," I told myself. "Forget it!" But the more I tried to forget, the more the idea intrigued me. As the minutes dragged by, the desire grew. What would it feel like to break a bone? What would happen? Would it bring more relief than cutting?

I sat on the red sofa, hands on my knees, each breath my only movement. The stillness of my body belied the racket in my head. The voices were so loud they were giving me a headache, and I was desperate to shut them up. I knew that only physical pain would silence the cacophony. Like ice cream on a hot day when you're on a diet, the hammer beckoned me. Just thinking about it gave me an eerie sense of calm.

I also knew, however, that giving in to this compulsion would drag me over some invisible line. I could just about manage the starving and cutting – but not broken bones. Part of it was practicality. How would I get to the hospital? I couldn't justify calling an ambulance for a self-inflicted injury, but I'd never be able to drive myself.

And how I would explain it as an accident? I worked through different scenarios in my head. I even got the stepladder out and set up a fake accident scene, but nothing seemed realistic enough to me. Had I stopped to think about it, I wouldn't have been able to imagine anything more unbelievable than a twenty-year-old girl smashing her leg with a hammer.

And the whole idea scared me. I had experience cutting and knew what I was doing, but hitting my leg with the hammer was completely different to anything I'd done before. I didn't know what would happen, but I knew it wouldn't be in my control. While that was part of what attracted me to the idea in the first place, the shred of common sense I was still able to muster told me that the unknown outcome made it a bad idea.

I never got the hammer out of the drawer. I knew that if I held it in my hand I wouldn't be able to resist, so I decided not to even look at it. Instead, I willed myself to pick up the phone and call Nikki, a friend who worked for a Christian eating disorder charity who had helped me through some difficult times the year before.

After just a few rings I heard her cheery voice say hello. I didn't want my dark desperation to cast its shadow over her, but I knew I had to say something to someone.

"Nikki it's Abbie I'm scared I'm at home and I've cut and I want to do more and I don't know what to do," I blurted out before I lost my nerve.

Nikki was as calm as I had known she would be. "What's going on, Abs? Has something set this off?" I could almost see her settling behind the desk with her big mug of tea, knowing that she'd be stuck to the phone for a while.

"I don't know. Nothing specific. It's just all too much. The biggest problem is just– just that I don't know." I could tell I wasn't making sense, but it was the best I could do.

"What's too much?" Nikki probed gently.

"Everything. Food. Eating. Feeling fat. Wanting to cut. Wanting to hurt myself more than ever before. Hating myself so much that I can't see straight. I don't know what I might do. It scares me."

There was a moment of silence and I could tell that Nikki wasn't sure what to say, I was in such a state. I desperately wanted to stop hurting myself, but at the same time I felt that I couldn't cope without it. I tried to explain to Nikki how I was feeling.

"It's like there's panic and hatred pushing out from inside me. I want to rage and scream and shout it out, but it just stays inside. I feel like it's burning, battering away to get. But I can't let it. I don't know why, but I can't get angry. I can't cry. So when it's threatening to burst my body takes over and does it for me, before it's poisoned from the inside out."

Talking about it like this was exhausting, and as Nikki began to respond to what I'd said I started spacing out. She prayed, and she wanted me to pray with her, but I just couldn't get my mind to focus on her words. Although I was a Christian, I couldn't see how God could possibly step in and help me. I wanted to believe that praying worked, but it seemed so pointless.

"Nikki, if I'm going to stop myself from self-harm I need to do something with my hands. I need to have something to concentrate on."

"Well," she said, "you write, don't you? You've always written things, as long as I've known you. You need to start getting it out of yourself, Abs. Try writing. Write whatever comes into your head. It will keep your hands busy, and you never know what you might discover in the process."

We promised to get together and talk again soon, and I agreed that I'd try to write what I was feeling. When I hung up the phone, the silence rang in my ears.

I found a notepad and pen and sat staring at the lines on the page. Where would I start? One small scribble got the ink flowing, and once I started it was hard to stop. Writing was cathartic, and not nearly as difficult as I'd expected. The following is what flowed from my pen that day:

It's hard to remember and describe how I feel before I cut. I think it starts with a feeling of being unsettled and unable to sit still. I wander aimlessly and everything seems out of focus. Everything passes over me, but it's not a relaxed or easy feeling – I'm trapped inside my head and everything outside is unreal. I feel claustrophobic, and it makes me panic because I can't escape.

Once I'm there inside my head, I can't get far enough out to interact with anyone else. I run out of patience – the idea of sitting and talking about what's wrong is laughable. I feel a burning need to alleviate the pressure before something out of my control happens.

When I do cut it's a relief – a sudden release of pressure like when you let go of the opening of a balloon to stop it bursting. Except that the pressure is the pain in my head, and the only thing that will relieve it is pain in my body.

I want the pain in my head to stop, but these days, no matter how much I cut, it doesn't. I don't know where the pain comes from, but I know that a lot of it is hatred of myself. It's so strong inside that I'm scared of letting it out. I can't show so much anger and pain, so the screams swirl around inside my head, driving me over the edge. I have to cut all the pain away, cut away the surface so I can escape what's inside of me.

I don't know how I'd live without cutting, what I'd do to survive. These people who ask if I am trying to kill myself have got it all wrong – it's just a survival method to get me through each day. It's not to die, it's to stay alive.

Writing down how I felt was very therapeutic – it was as if I was cutting at the paper with my pen. I pressed hard and scratched the coffee table, but I didn't break my leg with a hammer.

No one ever read what I wrote that day. I folded the piece of paper as small as I could, put it in a box, and vowed never to show it to anyone. I was petrified that people would never talk to me again if they knew just how crazy I really was. Maybe if I had let someone read it I would have received help and understanding, but I didn't want to risk losing anyone in my life.

Not long after that day, I began to see the insanity of what I was doing and I completely fell apart. I had to give up my job and move back home with my parents, and I only just managed to stay out of hospital by smiling sweetly and saying the things I knew the doctors wanted to hear. I curled up as small as I possibly could, said as little as I could get away with, and watched the grey world go by. Life was a happiness that eluded me, and I gave up searching.

2

"It's wonderful – you'll hate it," my dad told my mother.

That was the first she heard of our new house, and his words turned out to be truer than we could have imagined.

The mustiness enveloped me as soon as I walked through the door and into the gloom. The three-storey Victorian townhouse had come down in the world, and had been used most recently as a squat. The ceiling was so high I couldn't see it. I clung to my mother's leg and wondered if the place was haunted. My little brother David, though, squealed with toddler delight and sprinted down the long passageway towards the back of the house. Mum set off after him, but I stood in the doorway, hesitating.

"Come on, Abbie," Dad held out his hand. "Let's have a look around." He led me into the front room. The big windows were so dirty that the whole room was in darkness even on this early evening in August. I could just make out piles of rotting mattresses and old blankets. I wrinkled my nose and squeezed Dad's hand.

"It's scary – I don't want to bring my toys and books in here. It smells funny."

"It will be lovely once we've cleaned it up. Think of it as an adventure."

"I think I like clean adventures better, Daddy," I said.

As usual, what my father saw was not exactly what everyone else saw. My mother would have been perfectly justified in refusing to consider the house, but she could see potential lingering under the surface of mildew and dust. The hovel became home, and I spent the best part of my life there.

❁   ❁   ❁   ❁

My parents met at college, where they were both studying to be teachers. They taught in North London and then moved to Hertfordshire when they decided to start a family. When I finally arrived, three weeks overdue and following over fifty hours of labor, my parents' relief was only exceeded by their joy. The photo albums in my parents' house tell the story of every new thing I did – playing, smiling and tottering through my first steps – a normal, happy baby growing into a little girl.

When I was two and a half, my whole world turned upside down. I was introduced to a strange creature I was told was my little brother David. He shouted before he could talk, and ran before he walked. These chapters of the photo albums tell a slightly different story. The adults look more tired, and you can often spot stray hands in the corners of photographs, trying to keep David in one place.

I was the "good" child – in contrast to David, who was forever causing havoc. But although David had a penchant for trouble, it never prevented my mother from planning exciting activities for us to do together. While my dad was at work the three of us would enjoy doing all sorts of projects – making gingerbread men and finger painting – until David brought on a new disaster.

"I'll be with you in a minute, Abbie!" Mum shouted over her shoulder as she hurtled off down the hall after

David, who was spreading blue poster paint on the newly hung wallpaper. By the time she returned, I had finished my masterpiece and was ready to make my escape, back upstairs to my books.

"No Abbie," Mum called after me, "you need to help me put everything away. When you make the mess, you must help clean it up!"

I made a humphing noise. "David made more mess than me, and he never helps," I thought darkly.

Even as a toddler I was independent and self-sufficient rather than cuddly and talkative. I loved books and read from an early age, and what I couldn't read I made up.

One day, Mum came into my room while I was reading. Dad had built me bunk beds, and I was sitting on the top bunk with my books, a sanctuary from the noise David was making downstairs. Mum stuck her head around the door.

"What are you doing, darling?"

"I'm reading." I was short with my answer, too busy to involve myself in conversation.

"Can I sit with you and read?"

"No, I'm alright."

"Can I come up for a cuddle, then?"

"No, I'm trying to read. What does this word say?"

Mum came over and looked where I was pointing.

"It says 'because.' Do you want to read it to me?"

It was too late. I was engrossed again, creating worlds in my head where gingerbread men marched in a band and little girls flew over the earth by moonlight in toy boats.

Because I was four years old when we moved I was too young to start school but really too old for playgroup. But, since David went to playgroup, I went along with him.

"Can I write children's names on their paintings, please?" I asked the leader.

"Why don't you do another painting yourself, Abbie?" she replied.

"Because I've done one, and I don't want to do more. I do lots of paintings at home."

Mrs. Becker was bemused. "What if you can't spell the children's names, Abbie? You wouldn't want to get them wrong, would you?"

"No, but if you give me the register I could copy them. Then I'd be helping." Mrs. Becker gave me the sheet of paper and I wandered off to be helpful. While I'm sure Mrs. Becker didn't quite know what to do with me, I think I was aware at some level that I had more in common with grownups than with other children. Although I didn't begin to speak until I was older than most children, my first word was "mummy" and my second was "I don't want any more of that, thank-you." I yearned to counteract my boredom by engaging in proper, meaningful conversations. I loved to hold heated debates, but my arguments sounded wrong from a four-year-old's mouth.

❀   ❀   ❀   ❀

One of the best parts about moving to this house closer to London was being closer to the Morris folk dancing group my parents had founded. David and I would go with them to the Sunday rehearsals and learn the dances with the adults. Most weekends, especially in the summer, we would do performances and people would gush over the little ones dancing.

David showed a particular aptitude for dancing, and my parents encouraged this activity as a channel for all his energies. He never stopped.

In the kitchen while mum was cooking dinner, he would say to me, "Go over to that corner to dance and do what I do. But I do it first!" And, if I wanted to keep him from tearing around and injuring me, I would have to follow his lead – and so would Mum and Dad.

When he was five, a friend of the family wrote to the producers of the television show "That's Life," suggesting that they follow up on the story of the world's youngest Morris dancer. We went to an idyllic country pub to film various shots of David and the rest of the Morris men, including interviews with my parents. I had no part in the filming. I don't know whether it was because David was a better dancer, because he was smaller and cuter, because it was more unusual to see a little boy dancing, or because he'd inherited our dad's natural talent for performing. I sat under a tree outside the pub, playing dolls with another little girl whose mum was looking after me while my parents were busy inside. At one point the sound engineer came over, waving his large, furry microphone.

"What's your name?" he asked.

"Abbie," I answered, flashing a gappy grin.

"Well, Abbie," he said, "you're a very pretty little girl." I smiled to myself as he went back to where the action was, flattered by the attention. Later I sought him out and he let me sing into one of his microphones. When he told me I had a pretty voice I decided I might be a singer when I grew up.

But David was the focus of all the attention once the show was broadcast. It was a hit, and people would come up to us on the street to talk to the little Morris boy. His photo was in the local papers during the summer months of dance, and David loved every minute of it.

This was the first of many times I was to stand in my brother's shadow. He excelled and collected awards in ballet as well as Morris dancing, cricket and drama. He shouted loudly and stood tall and I stood silent in the wings, clapping, but all the while feeling jealous and a little bit sad.

It often seemed as though Morris dancing was all we did through the summers. Other people got to see us more than we got to see each other, and Dad was so busy entertaining everyone else that there was very little left over for us.

Dad was full of nervous energy – he was thin and wiry with wild hair and a crazy beard that grew in all directions. Gregarious by nature, he was never happier than when he was surrounded by people. During our dance performances Dad always played the role of the Fool – a traditionally comical character whose job it is to attract and hold the attention of the crowd. He relished this role and performed all the time – whether in costume or not. He was at his most comfortable when he was fooling.

He would stride out into the middle of the festival or pub garden where we were dancing and shout in his booming voice, "Welcome to sunny, exotic Enfield!" Huge crowds would follow us because Dad was such a good entertainer. People would exclaim about how wonderful he was, and children would come up to me and say, "I wish he was my dad."

I remember my dad best the way he was around other people – usually entertaining them in some way. It was important to him to be loved and well thought of, and he would often have been out doing things to help others. He would always be the life of the party – juggling salt shakers in a restaurant or singing while walking down the street. He even pretended to propose to my mum on one knee in the supermarket with a head of broccoli. I thought he was great when we were out, but this wasn't the same dad who lived at home with us. Suddenly and unpredictably, he would lose his temper and the laughter would turn to shouting. Meal times were the worst. One day a spilled glass of water would be mopped up without comment, another day the same accident would trigger an outburst. His anger would abate almost immediately, but while it lasted it was terrifying. We all learned to make allowances during those brief periods when he was at home instead of working.

While my dad was the storm, my mum was the reliable yardstick by which we could measure everything. We could rely on her to always react in the way we expected. She might not have given us enthusiastic congratulations, unexpected presents or surprise outings the way Dad did, but we knew with her that we didn't have to worry about over-the-top arguments or extreme emotions.

❀   ❀   ❀   ❀

I began my educational career in the school where my mum was a teacher. In my first week, I got a special mention in school assembly. Mrs. Hutchins announced the names of the children who had achieved something praiseworthy that week.

"And our special mentions today are: Oliver, for getting all his sums right, Heidi, for drawing this beautiful garden, and Abbie, because she put all her brushes back into the right saucers every single time so the paints didn't get mixed."

A noble act, you may agree, but all I could think as I walked up to the podium was that my painting wasn't good enough. Any idiot could tell their colors apart. I may have received a chocolate bar and a smattering of applause when I got to the front, but I didn't have a piece of work to hold up. That feeling stayed with me throughout my years there.

I met Sarah on the first day of school, and from that moment on we were inseparable. I didn't need anyone else. Although we looked very different and enjoyed different subjects, we both loved books and often talked only when it was necessary to share a specific witticism. When the other girls talked about hair and dolls, I never quite managed to join in.

"We're going to play families," Helen would say. "I'm the mummy. You're small, Abbie – you can be the baby."

"Can Sarah and I bring our books out so Sarah can pretend to read to me?" I'd ask. But they'd moved on to persuading Daniel to be the dad. I sighed. I didn't really want to play families anyway.

The best playtimes were the ones after I fell down the stairs and broke my arm. "You can sit outside the office," Miss Jones said. "Sarah can stay in with you. Why don't you choose a book from the library to read?" I was in my element.

When I started school I also started Sunday school. I'm not quite sure why my parents sent me, because they never went to church themselves, but my early church experience was very positive. I loved getting dressed up in pretty dresses and enjoyed reading Bible stories and making things with my friends. In Scripture classes we studied the Bible and took exams every year. Although I did well on the exams, I never thought that what I learned was anything more than stories to be memorized. I certainly didn't know that the Bible had anything to do with my life.

Through church I met Karen, with whom I would have a love-hate relationship for 15 years. Although she was my friend, there were times I didn't like her at all. When I had 10 brownie badges, she had 20; when I passed my Grade 3 violin exam, she passed Grade 6. Everything I could do, she could do better. She was a year ahead of me in school, even though she was a month younger, so she experienced everything first. Second best, I chased after her shadow. But I also loved her dearly most of the time. In later years we shared our angst and struggles and were slightly odd together, isolated from the rest of our worlds.

❋   ❋   ❋   ❋

When I was ten, I discovered the cathartic nature of pain for the first time.

During playtime at school, another child ran to tell me, "David's cut his lip, like, really badly! I think he might die! He's so bleeding!"

Caring sister that I was, I ran as fast as I could (which wasn't very fast) to get help. I got as far as the front door, fell over the doormat and dug a huge chunk out of my knee. David's injury turned out to be hardly more than a scratch – lips bleed profusely for very little reason. My own wound was more serious – not a scratch that could be fixed with a bandage and a kiss, but rather a big chunk of flesh hanging on for dear life by a thread of scuffed, dirty skin. No one seemed to know what to do with it. I sat and looked calmly at the waxy white bit of knee, wondering if that small part of me was now dead. The playground attendants on duty obviously thought not, because it was pushed back into its hole and covered with a bandage. Teachers congratulated me for being good, for not crying, for being brave. The other kids were just impressed by how big the bandage was. I hardly heard. I couldn't stop thinking about my knee being dead, and I wondered how long it would take for the rest of me to follow. As I wandered around the playground, pretending to play, I felt a panic creeping over me. I kept pinching myself because I had read that that's what you do to make sure you aren't dreaming. I hadn't read any books about dying yet, but I was pretty sure pinching would work to abate that too.

When the bell finally rang, I was ushered into the school office to wait until the nurse came back. As I sat in the enormous black chair reserved for sick people, my whole body quivered with anxiety. I didn't really see Mrs. Farley cleaning my wound with a wet piece of tissue, and I heard her as if from a great distance when she told me it might hurt a little. She poked around and squeezed water over the gritty little hole and its dangling cork.

My newly undead knee screamed with pain. I snapped back to reality and began to breathe again. The school office was filled with an exquisite sense of calm, and my head stopped ringing. All was silent.

3

Everything felt different.

I vividly recall the power of that moment but I could not then, nor can I now, articulate exactly what had made it so profound. Everything appeared to make more sense. The pain I felt seemed almost spiritual, and I felt every physical sensation in a new way.

It didn't occur to me that I could do to myself what Mrs. Farley had done for me. I didn't understand my anxiety, or how the pain had pulled me back. I didn't need to hold on to the memory of it, either. I was only ten – I didn't need an escape route back to reality. All I knew was that I was alive, and that was good. I became fascinated by what made me alive – what it was beneath my skin that made me human. I wanted to explore my body and started gouging holes in my arms with my fingernails. I wasn't trying to create pain or achieve the same sensation. I just wanted to see what was there.

Somehow I knew that my parents wouldn't approve of these explorations, or the thoughts I was having about my body. I could imagine their what-a-silly-girl look and feel their rejection. So I kept it secret.

I couldn't wait to leave the school I'd outgrown and step out into the big bad world. Although I liked to know my surroundings and felt safe where I was, I also craved change. I started changing small things in my life whenever I wasn't happy with what else was happening around me, reinventing myself with different color schemes in my bedroom, or a new haircut. I began a new journal every couple of months. Every first page said, "I'm starting a new chapter in my life . . ."

I wrote stories in my journals featuring myself as the heroine in exotic places surrounded by new friends with whom I would have exciting adventures. Every evening I escaped into an imaginary, perfect world in the pages of a hard-backed notebook. There I became someone I liked more than the real me.

Stories from the summer of 1990 explore the theme of starting a new school, where I would be bright and witty and wow everyone with my charm and good looks. I drew a little confidence from this picture of myself as the perfect student. Outside these stories, in the real world, I was petrified of not being able to live up to the standards I thought would be imposed on me.

❀　　❀　　❀　　❀

As I stood at the bus stop, surrounded by people who seemed much older and full of confidence, I cursed Dad for refusing to drive me to school in the car.

"You'll have to get used to the bus, you might as well start now," he said as he left me on my own. No one else looked new, and I was certain everyone knew that I didn't belong.

The knot in my stomach tightened as the bus chugged along. At each stop more and more strangers filled the seats around me. I ran through lists in my head. I had my pencil case, my lunch money and my blank notebooks. My bag was the required navy blue, and I was wearing the right uniform. I couldn't think of any reason why I would look as out of place as I felt. I chewed at my nails, certain I'd get lost as soon as we arrived at school.

My biggest fear was allayed as I followed the herd of other new students to our assembly. I gazed longingly down the corridors at older students who were greeting each other with such ease and familiarity. They were so comfortable and confident. I couldn't wait to look like that, and excitement gradually replaced my anxiety as I thought about the community I was about to become a part of.

I was almost quietly confident as I settled into my first class. History. Pen poised over empty notebook, I waited.

"Right," the teacher said. "Can anyone tell me . . ."

And I was lost. I looked helplessly as hands all around me shot up. I had no idea what he was talking about. I felt so stupid. I realized that I would never fit in – everyone else was cleverer and picked things up much more easily then me. I was useless.

The rest of my classes were easier, but the history lesson stuck in my head all day. I couldn't stop telling myself off for being stupid. I was so desperate to do well that any suggestion of weakness terrified me. I resolved to work extra hard at the subjects like history that I hadn't studied as much.

But, as the days went by, I found lots of new and exciting things to get involved in – dance club, choir, orchestra and drama club. I'd been hearing how good the school was for so long that I felt it was my duty to take part in everything. I loved all the activity, and I was energized by the buzz of self-discovery.

I also discovered for the first time a whole world of people and concerns outside North London. I wanted to help others and became involved in the charities group. I wrote letters for Amnesty International and helped organize fundraisers for different groups helping children. Although I was aware of being part of a corrupt human race, I also felt deeply and personally responsible for the plights of others.

One day, I was approached by an older student from the charities group.

"We've decided to do the twenty-four-hour famine set up by World Vision to help send aid to third-world countries. Do you want to do it?"

I almost looked around to check she was talking to me. "What, go without food for twenty-four hours? I suppose. Do we get people to pledge money for it?"

"That's the idea. Can you publicize it with the other new students? The more people we get to do it, the better."

I nodded and she handed me a pile of sponsor forms.

"Thanks, kid," she smiled. As I watched her rejoin her friends, I felt pride that I'd been asked to help.

As the famine date grew closer, I got more and more animated about the cause. I couldn't wait for the day to arrive when I would actually be doing something so practical. I hassled everyone I knew, passionately proclaiming the good work that their donations would make possible. Throughout those twenty-four hours of fasting I tried to imagine what it must be like to go without food every day, but my imagination couldn't quite stretch that far. The gravity of the situation hit me hard, and I became very serious. I was relieved that I could do something practical and useful to help, and I felt that I was really making a difference. Although I raised more money than anyone else in the school for the famine, I didn't seek or want accolades for that. What mattered to me was that, despite feeling unlikeable and stupid, I could actually be of real help to someone else.

That feeling of achievement I enjoyed from going without something so central to everyday life became a driving force in my life. I began to skip lunch every time I wanted anything particular for someone else. Whenever I heard about a newly taken hostage, or an oil spill, or when one of my friends was upset, I would go without food for the school day – martyring myself for them so that they weren't alone in their suffering. I had never come across the Christian practice of fasting, and I never associated it with God, but I did it religiously from then on – just to feel that I was of some use to someone.

Being involved with music also boosted my confidence, as our school toured different countries and won national and international competitions. I loved being in the orchestra and choir and looked forward to every rehearsal. My days were so full that I often didn't have time to eat lunch – even when I wasn't on one of my fasts for a worthy cause. Doing worthwhile things was much more important to me than stopping for food, and I felt like I'd achieved something each lunchtime by the work I put in to everything I did. Although I never excelled academically, my teachers and fellow students saw a bright, bubbly and enthusiastic student, easy going but conscientious.

I enjoyed the arts subjects most, and especially English. I could read and call it homework! I loved anything that wasn't based on real life and inhabited each fictional world. I especially enjoyed creative writing because I could escape even further, making up my own worlds where everything was perfect. My plotlines read like tabloid magazines – illness, death and hardship, but, inevitably, triumph through adversity. My first-person heroines were either popular and talented or surviving gracefully and bravely in tragic situations. I dreamed of being an author and planned teenage dramas that would shoot me into fame, but I didn't consider who would read my tales of woe. I never showed my parents these stories because I didn't want them to know that I was considering such sadness. I wanted to remain in their minds the happy, bubbly daughter they knew.

All my stories were sad – completely disconnected from the fun and active life I was living and enjoying. I romanticized suffering and pain although I'd never really experienced either. But I felt like I knew my characters, and I related to them more easily than I did to my peers. While my reality was ordinary and boring, my stories gave me an outlet for expressing the unexplained sadness I felt a lot of the time. It never occurred to me to ask why I felt the way I did, or to strive to achieve a feeling of contentment in real life.

❀　　❀　　❀　　❀

I really felt like I belonged when I walked into school on the first day of my second year. As I walked to my first class I spotted a group of new students and realized I had become one of those older students I'd envied only a year ago. I greeted friends and checked the notice boards so that I knew what was happening.

I walked into my classroom and looked around for an extra seat. The desks had been in rows the previous year, but here they were grouped in tables of six. The only empty seat was a lone desk at the back. Frantically I scanned the room for friends from last year to see if someone was beckoning me to a saved seat, but everyone was deep in conversation. I stood at the door feeling crushed.

The teacher walked up behind me. "Sit down somewhere, will you Abbie?"

"Will the tables be staying like this, Sir?" I asked, my voice tremulous.

"We'll work it out later if you're not happy. But there's too much to do this morning, so just find a seat anywhere."

I wandered to the sad-looking desk at the back, and started putting my things inside. I waited for someone to turn around and say hi, but no one ever did. I got a book out of my bag and tried to look busy. I was determined not to show how disappointed and lonely I felt.

The teacher never did change the desks around, and I never had the confidence to ask again. If people don't want to sit with me they must know something I don't, I reasoned. I sat at my lone desk, sticking out like a blemish and trying to be invisible.

As the school year went on it got worse, and I ended up sitting on my own for every class. I was always the last to be picked for team quizzes, and physical education was a nightmare I dreaded each Thursday as I found myself standing alone in the field, flanked by two groups of teenaged girls who thought their teams were complete without me. It wasn't that they were horrible to me; they just didn't notice me or want me around. I learned to steer clear of people and I avoided speaking in front of others at all costs. Whenever I was called upon to answer a question I put my hand over my mouth as I talked and slouched down in my chair. My classmates laughed at me whether the answer was right or not.

I was completely isolated, caught up in a vicious cycle of feeling unworthy. I had low self-esteem because I had no friends, but I felt unable to try and make friends because my self-esteem was so low! I felt enveloped in a visible cloud that warned people I was to be avoided. I'm not sure if it began with one individual culprit or whether there was a group exodus away from me, but the hurt was excruciating. Sunday School wasn't much better, as my low confidence stopped me from talking to anyone unless I had to. I soon left the church for good. I couldn't see the point – I didn't have as many friends, the choir had folded and it was boring. Had I known anything of God in a personal way I might have stuck it out, but as it was, at thirteen I had better things to do with my Sunday mornings.

I couldn't talk to anyone about what was going on or how I felt about it – I didn't know how. Each day seemed longer than the one before as I battled with the loneliness that had been forced upon me. I couldn't understand why no one wanted to be my friend. Was I really that bad a person? And it had all been so sudden – what had happened to me over the summer that had made me so undesirable? It had to be me – my classmates couldn't all have changed so much in a few months.

None of my teachers seemed to notice that I was always alone. I worried that my parents might find out that I was an outcast when they got my first report that year, but nothing was said about it. I was still achieving academically, so as far as the school was concerned everything was fine. At the time I was relieved – I didn't want them to know what was going on. But part of me did wish that I could be open about the torment I was going through rather than pretending that everything was fine. I didn't want to worry them, disappoint them or tarnish their image of me as the model daughter.

Things got slightly better as that year went on. Another girl was ostracized, and I found myself with a new friend. Slowly, a small group formed around us, and I was no longer the class leper. But those months left an indelible mark on me. From that point on I considered having friends to be a complete fluke. I didn't deserve people to like me, and I began an unrelenting process of self-scrutinizing, looking for areas of my personality I could change in order to make myself more likeable.

4

"Will you go out with me?"

The question shocked me so much that I looked around the cold March school ground to check that he didn't mean someone else. No one else was around, so I weighed up the options in my head. On the one hand, Tom was somewhat antisocial and people thought he was a bit strange – he wasn't the kind of boyfriend I'd imagined for myself. On the other hand, I did kind of like him – even if not in the way I had imagined – and we liked a lot of the same things. The choice became clearer as I realized that the options were either having a boyfriend or not having one.

"Sure," I said. "That'd be cool."

The relationship that was born on that momentous occasion was not the kind I had imagined, but it was better than nothing. We walked around school holding hands and walked partway home together. We didn't kiss, and we barely talked. We just walked.

I wanted to have a boyfriend so I could be like other girls and at least appear to be worth as much as them. I was also one of the last girls I knew to have a boyfriend and wanted to get this rite of passage out of the way. But I felt guilty for not wanting to be with Tom for the right reasons. I took relationships very seriously, and I didn't want the responsibility of making a relationship work, so I kept Tom at arm's length.

Surprisingly, it lasted much longer than most "relationships" at that age, and by the following November we were still together. One blustery night he was invited to a party, and I tagged along for fun. And fun it was – that evening I had my first real kiss. It was the most romantic moment in the world. We were slow dancing to Madonna's "Crazy For You," the lights were dimmed, and people clapped. Thinking about it now, it had its downsides – the braces tangled, the in-crowd laughed and he stepped on my feet. But it was soft and wet and all-encompassing – everything a kiss should be. It was the only one we had.

One of the good things about being with Tom was that I made some new friends. When we walked home, we would tag along with Tom's older brother and his friends. I wanted to be like them – they were all terribly flamboyant and had conversations about the state of the world that I had trouble following. My friends seemed dull in comparison, and I wished that I was older and that they saw me as an equal, not as the hanger-on girlfriend of the kid brother. Even Tom outdid me in the eccentric intellectuality I desperately wanted.

Tom and I lasted for a whole nine months, after which I decided I'd had enough. Following what seemed like a very civilized break-up, just like in the adult romance books I read, he wrote me a letter. He wrote that I was frigid, dull and boring and that I had been a complete waste of nine months of his life because I wouldn't get my knickers down. I accepted it all as fact, but I didn't really care one way or the other. I pretended to be upset and indignant about what he had said to me, and disgusted that he had wanted nothing but sex. But I was as bored as he was, and I missed spending lunchtime with my friends.

The only problem was that I desperately wanted to stay friends with the older crowd we walked home from school with. The way to do that, I decided, was to keep walking home with them. I just kept my distance from Tom and avoided eye contact. The best part of that walk home was the last bit, when only Lizzie and I were left. Lizzie was a cheery and outgoing artist with an inane sense of humor. She also had a take on the world that I'd never encountered and didn't understand. She talked about her Christian faith and described some of the aspects of what she believed that shaped her life. We also talked about relationships, and she comforted me after the split with Tom.

Although Lizzie always listened to me and never made me feel like anything I said wasn't worth saying, I was constantly worried that she and the rest of the group would ditch me as soon as they discovered how boring I was. They cared for me and gave me the attention I craved, and I was desperate not to lose that. I had to figure out a way to keep their friendship. So I decided to become anorexic.

The causes and sustaining factors of eating disorders are incredibly complex, which is partly why they are so difficult to treat and recover from. But I can say, without a doubt, that mine started because I wanted to be noticed. I wanted an excuse to tell people that I was sad, and I wanted to make sure that people wouldn't stop being my friends. Although there were many contributing factors, I categorically *decided* to become anorexic. My eating disorder was, from the start, my method of manipulation. Only later would it become an addiction I had to break.

❀   ❀   ❀   ❀

I peeked around the classroom door, trying to see whether Tina and her gang were in there. Sometimes they didn't spot me and I could escape to kill time in the music room until the bell rang for class to start. When they weren't there I could sit down and chat with someone in peace. But usually one of her little group spotted me and pointed me out.

"Hey Abbie!" she yelled as I cringed. "Had any breakfast this morning? I'd skip it if I were you – you don't want to make that backside of yours any bigger!"

The girls around her sniggered as I walked as calmly as possible to my desk. She wasn't very original and never said anything that could get her into real trouble. If it wasn't my body it was my lack of boyfriend or that I wasn't as smart as other people or that I should wear a bag over my head.

I never thought of it as bullying. Lots of people put up with jibes from the more popular crowd – I was just one of many they belittled on a regular basis. They never hit me or kicked me or stole my lunch money. They just whispered as I walked past them or stuck notes on my desk telling me I was useless.

I was an easy target. I never stood up to them – partly because, for the most part, I agreed with them. I was fat and ugly and stupid, and nobody in their right mind would like me. My self-esteem was already low – they just pounded at it until there was very little left. I knew there was very little I was good at, and I agreed I'd probably be better off giving up right there and then. I did try a few times to tell my teacher what was going on, but Ms. Smith ignored me. When comments were made I'd look at her, hoping she'd put a stop to it, but she just smirked.

At the beginning of my fifth year of secondary school I was anxiety-ridden, insecure and afraid to try anything new. One thing that kept me going was being able to sing, and I eventually plucked up my courage to audition for the school play. Having assumed I'd failed the audition, I was surprised and ecstatic to be offered the lead role in a musical I loved – Maria in *West Side Story*. I wasn't at all sure I'd be able to do it, but my music teacher, Miss Ambrose, kept telling me she had faith in me. And, over time, I started to believe her. I looked forward to the daily rehearsals more than anything else, and I immersed myself in learning lines and choreography.

One day, a lunch-time rehearsal ran overtime. Although I'd never been late before, I knew that lateness was one of Ms. Smith's pet peeves. As I ran to class I wondered whether I would get the frown everyone else got, or whether there would be more serious consequences. I walked through the door apologizing.

"I'm sorry, I was in the drama hall rehearsing and the bell doesn't ring in there and we lost track of time and Mr. Vickers says he's sorry it's his fault and . . ." My words fell over each other as Ms. Smith glared. She pointed to a spot in front of the blackboard.

"Stand there," she spat.

Silently, I obeyed.

Ten minutes later, as the class was filing out, I was still standing there. Ms. Smith sat and stared at me. I looked down at the floor.

"You were late."

"Yes. Mr. Vickers said not to blame me, to talk to him about it." I gave her a pleading glance.

She looked me up and down. "Making the usual excuses, I see. I don't know why you bother – I know what you're like. What makes an irresponsible little girl think she can answer back to a teacher?"

I was shamed into silence and hung my head, waiting for the diatribe to finish.

"You're not as special as you think you are – you're just a stupid, homely little girl who thinks she's outside the rules."

I tried to look her in the eye without showing how much I was quaking.

"Detention on Thursday. I don't care about your rehearsals – I'll see you in detention. And you won't be doing homework. I want you writing lines."

She fired her parting shot as she swept past me and out the door, so close that her skirt swished against my legs.

"I don't know why they put you in that school play. It's not like you're going to be any good."

I leaned against the wall and dissolved in tears. Part of me knew she was just a bully who would say anything to upset me, but the questions still ricocheted around in my head. Was she right? Was I really homely? Was I really irresponsible? And, most importantly, was I really going to be terrible in the play?

I stumbled blindly down the corridor towards my next class. I felt triumphant that I hadn't cried in front of Ms. Smith, but now I couldn't stop. Everyone was in their classroom by now, so there was no one to see the tears. I almost smiled at the bitter irony of the fact that I was now late for my first afternoon class.

"Abbie?" My music teacher caught my arm as she walked past. I hadn't even noticed her coming. "What's wrong?"

"I . . . Ms . . ." The tears started again. Miss Ambrose took my arm and led me to her office at the end of the corridor. She sat me down with a box of tissues and listened quietly as I told her exactly what had happened.

"I'll see what I can do. Are you okay to go to your next class?"

"I suppose so. What does my face look like?"

"You look fine. I'll see you at rehearsal later, alright?"

I nodded and headed to German, wondering what was going to happen. All I wanted to do was go home, curl up in a ball and never come to school again.

I didn't see Ms. Smith for the rest of the day, which was a relief. As the week passed I waited for something to be done about Ms. Smith, but nothing ever was. Nothing changed, and I decided the rest of the year would be easier to endure if I gave up hoping that it would.

West Side Story was sold-out, and everyone who saw it seemed to love it. I sang my heart out every night. By the end of the week I was exhausted, but exhilarated. And yet, I still couldn't get the doubts out of my head. I found it so much harder to accept praise than negative comments. Despite encouragement from my parents, Miss Ambrose and my friends, it was what people like Ms. Smith and Tina and her friends said that stuck in my mind. Over the year, I calmly accepted that I was a complete waste of space. I couldn't do anything well, and I was somehow managing to fool all my friends into thinking I was likeable. They just hadn't found out that, somewhere along the line, I had become a bad person.

❀   ❀   ❀   ❀

Although I tried hard, I wasn't very good at being anorexic. One day I would be surviving on a staple diet of oranges, the next wolfing down one of my mum's delicious dinners because I was so hungry and liked meat so much. I became obsessed with food but never lost very much weight and could never stick to a diet for very long. I would often use food – or lack of it – to cope when things were difficult, but it wasn't chronic. The frustrating thing was that people weren't noticing, so it wasn't getting me what I really wanted – love and attention. I tried to tell people about my struggles with food, but they never took me seriously enough to keep asking how I was.

"Perhaps if I'm thinner they'll notice," I kept thinking. So I would starve myself a little bit longer, and perhaps even skip dinner. But it turned out that I had the metabolism of a camel, so I never lost what I saw as my "spare" weight. The family photo albums are full of pictures of a happy – if slightly skinny – young girl. But in the mirror I saw someone so utterly unlikable that she didn't deserve food – which made not eating easier than ever.

❀   ❀   ❀   ❀

One night, at youth club, I was sitting on the floor and chatting with my friend Karen about the stress of the impending exams. Because I was so nervous about the practice exams coming up, I babbled on and on. She was quieter than usual and sat looking down at the floor.

"Are you okay?" I asked her. She opened her mouth as if to speak, but no words came out. Instead, she pulled up her sleeve to reveal rows of scratches on her forearm.

"What happened?" I asked. I was trying to figure out what kind of accident could have caused them.

"Nothing happened," she said in a monotone. "I did them." She got up and walked away. As I watched her go, I tried to figure out what she meant. Was she saying she scratched her arm on purpose? When people cut their arms, I thought, they're usually trying to kill themselves. Had Karen attempted suicide? I followed Karen out to the bathroom, where she was sitting behind the door.

"I thought you'd probably follow me," she said. She looked worn and tired.

"I don't understand. You cut your own arms? Were you trying to kill yourself?" She looked at me as if I was crazy.

"Don't you think if I wanted to kill myself I'd make more than a few scratches? I'm not stupid."

I was the one who felt stupid for not understanding. "What then? Why did you do it?"

"It just helps me feel better, that's all."

I just stared, uncomprehending and a bit frightened.

"I cut myself because I don't like myself and because I'm sad. When I feel bad I can't concentrate on anything else. I can't listen to conversations or study or anything. So I cut to help me concentrate." She sounded very matter-of-fact.

"I don't get it."

"It's like I space out, and I can't really hear anything or understand anything. It's scary, because I don't know what's going to happen and I feel completely out of control. So I cut, and then I'm back in the land of the living and I can concentrate on things again and I know that I'm in control of how I feel. I know it sounds crazy, but it works."

"But doesn't everyone feel like that sometimes?" I asked. "I feel like that all the time – I'm always trying to keep up with what's going on so I don't completely space out and miss everything. I'm constantly trying to get rid of how I feel and ignore the panic attacks that are just about to blow. But I don't cut myself." I shook my head.

The whistle blew in the other room, calling us back to the meeting. Karen stood up and brushed off her skirt.

"Maybe you should," she said as she disappeared out the door.

I sat for a while longer, staring into space. Maybe Karen was right. Maybe I should.

A few weeks later, sitting in English class, I felt myself begin to space out. I kept getting halfway through sentences, unable to complete them. I was trying so hard to concentrate, because I wanted to do well on my exams, but then all of a sudden I heard my teacher snap at me to pay attention, and I realized that I had no idea what he'd just said. I remembered what Karen had said. Maybe causing myself physical pain could really keep me grounded enough to concentrate for a whole class.

I pulled up the sleeves of my jumper and began to pinch my arms, leaving little half crescent dips where my nails punctured the skin. And, all of a sudden, things were clear. Voices weren't muffled any more, and I could concentrate on everything that was being said. It was like a miracle cure – just one small pinch.

I never told anyone about my lost minutes, or about the way I dealt with them. I questioned my own sanity plenty of times, but I never thought to ask anyone else's advice. I became obsessed with the idea of cutting, and I was fascinated by the effect Karen had said it had, but I never tried it. Instead, I continued flirting with the idea by pinching myself hard enough to leave marks or scratching my skin over and over again, causing friction burns. I knew I could explain away marks caused by pinching and scratching, but cuts like Karen's would be impossible to lie about. I was tempted by the razor blades that Karen carried around in her purse, but I resisted the temptation – particularly after Karen's parents found out what she'd been doing and forced her to see a psychologist.

It occasionally occurred to me that what I was doing might be seen as weird, but I never thought of it as a symptom of the depression I was feeling. Nor did I think that if I told someone they might have given me the attention I craved. It was just something I did now and again as a means to an end. The physical sensation helped me concentrate – it improved my attention span and kept my mind from drifting off. The mild discomfort kept me anchored to the classroom and my notebook, able to follow entire lectures. It served a useful function.

During the semester I turned sixteen, it was my relationship with pain and hunger that kept me going until the big, end-of-year exams that would determine whether or not I could continue at school. When I was thinking about food or self-harm, I didn't have to worry about how good or bad I was at things. It took my mind off the fear of failure and the suspicion that no one liked me. The coping mechanisms I was polishing blanketed all my worries, and I managed to get through the rest of the school year without falling apart. I threw myself into my studies and actually felt capable of passing my exams.

When the exam days arrived I went to school, sat in the stifling hot hall, wrote until my arm ached, and left. The expanse of summer stretched out before me with endless possibilities. I sat around a lot, wrote a lot of bad poetry and busied myself with my reading list for the following year. I was determined that my final school exams would be completely different, and I would do so well that I could get into any university in the country. I had completely different teachers and I was only studying the subjects I really enjoyed – Music, English and Religious Studies. I would have different teachers so I wasn't going to have to cope with Ms. Smith, and I wouldn't have to see Tina and the other girls I wanted to avoid. I couldn't wait. My exam results arrived at the end of the summer. They were good, but only average compared to those of my classmates. I went back to school and threw myself in.

Two weeks after the beginning of the school year I got my first essay back, marked in red with a large "D." I entertained thoughts of suicide as I read through the "constructive" criticism, trying to keep the red "D" from clouding my view. The voices telling me I was stupid drowned my dreams of being the best senior student ever, and I started to work all hours just to keep up. So began my journey towards university, and so it continued.

5

Under the pressure of working towards the exams, I focused more and more on losing weight and self-harm. During a music department trip away I tried not to eat at all and began fainting at the most inopportune moments – usually during concerts. I was rewarded for this by being forced to sit with the teachers during meals. I sat there humiliated, picking at my food.

Once back, I managed to avoid this kind of mortification, but I still had to endure comments about how unhealthy I was being, and how much better I would feel if I ate like a good girl. No one ever asked what was really going on, or why I wasn't eating – and I never told them. Some teachers scolded me for not eating as if I were five years old, and I began to avoid anyone I thought might lecture me about eating. I didn't think it was such a big deal anyway – not when I compared myself to the skinny girls in the magazines I devoured. Depression washed over me in waves, and I felt isolated again.

During that music trip I had a long conversation with Lizzie about God. We sat on one of the top bunks in her room, sharing a bunch of grapes while most of the others were out partying.

"I'm just not sure he exists," I said. "It's not about proof – I know lots of philosophers thought up theories to prove God exists. It's about what God has to do with me, and why I would want to believe in him. It doesn't matter to me whether God created the world or will judge humanity – that has nothing to do with me personally. But you keep talking about having a relationship with God, and that's why it matters whether I believe in him, because it's an individual choice. Whether or not I want a relationship with *him*, what I can't understand is why he'd want a relationship with *me*." The arguments circled in my head, but they weren't becoming any clearer to me as I tried to explain what I'd been thinking about to Lizzie.

"If you believe in a God who created the world, then you have to admit that he would have done it for his own pleasure, right?" she asked.

I nodded.

"So, if you were created for his pleasure, it makes sense that he wants a relationship with you. He didn't create you to leave you to your own devices – he created you so he could love you and enjoy you. If he didn't want to have anything to do with you after creating you, it would be like baking a cake and then not eating it – the whole thing becomes pointless," Lizzie explained patiently.

I turned the idea over in my head. "Okay, I get that bit, I think. But the way I see it is that I've made a real mess of my life so far, and even if God wanted a relationship with the me he created, he wouldn't want the me I am now. How could he ever want a relationship with me, considering the mess I'm in?"

"Because he's like a father – the perfect kind – who always wants to be with his child. In the Bible there's a story of a son who took all his dad's money, went off and spent it all, led a real party life and ended up eating pig slop because he couldn't afford food. And yet, when he finally went home, his dad was desperate to see him, and literally ran down the road to meet him. That's how God feels about you – if you said you wanted a relationship with him, he'd run down the road to meet you."

I was quiet. I didn't get it at all. I hated myself, and I couldn't understand why on earth God would want me. Why was Lizzie spending time talking to me when she could be doing other things? I asked a tentative question.

"Let's say I might believe it when I know more, but I don't know yet. How would I go about knowing more?"

Lizzie sat back. "Probably by talking to all the people you know who do have a relationship with God, and by listening to what they say about him. And you could also go to church with me and see what you find out?"

I wasn't sure I wanted to go that far. I hadn't been to church for years and I didn't remember anything that was said there that was worth knowing. But Lizzie looked so hopeful, and it seemed so important to her that I give it some serious thought, that I agreed.

"Okay. But don't push me into anything, alright? I want to find out at my own pace."

The following Sunday, I went to church with Lizzie and found that I quite enjoyed it. I started going to an evening service with her each week and formed a group of friends with whom I found it easy to spend time. I stayed quiet and tried not to draw attention to myself, but these people cared for me and always took the time to ask my opinion on things. At school people expected me to do and achieve things to earn respect, but with my church friends there were no expectations. They respected me just for being me, and they valued my opinions. I felt more at home there than anywhere, and I settled quickly into the routine of church.

In the beginning, church was far more important to me than God, and I had been going to church for quite a while before the penny began to drop. Despite my Sunday school upbringing, I didn't understand what it really meant to be a Christian. I think as far as I was concerned I was already a Christian – I was born in England, I had been to church as a child, and I certainly wasn't anything else.

But hearing sermons every week, and singing songs about Christ that resonated with me, sowed the seeds of what it meant to have faith in God. The group of friends I was now a part of lived by example, and I listened in on all the conversations they had about faith and trust. I was also taking Religious Studies at school, and all of this began to answer questions about who I was – and it generated more questions as well.

After a few months, I was asked to sing with the worship group and people praised me both for my voice and for my commitment, which I loved. I felt valued for singing, and I was pleased that I could do something helpful by leading the congregation in song. One evening I was told that my voice was a gift. This experience opened my eyes to the reality of God, and I began to see much more clearly that he created me to be unique and that he cared for me despite the mistakes I made every day.

I had been going to church for about six months when I finally decided that I had to either accept it all or give it up completely. I felt like a hypocrite every time I came to church, taking the things I wanted from it without actually committing to it. I knew that the Bible was true with a certainty that I can't quite place. It was partly logical – nothing else made as much sense – but my real belief was actually far more intuitive. I just knew that I had no other choice but to live a life that was focused on God. So on 28 January 1996 I said a prayer that changed my life: "God, I want to live my life the way you want

me to, and I want to be in a relationship with you forever. I'm sorry I thought I could do better without you.
Please forgive me, and help me live the rest of my life for
you. Amen."

It wasn't a dramatic Damascus road experience. I
gave my life to God in a very quiet way on a very normal day. But, from that moment on, I knew my focus
had changed. And, more than anything else, I knew that
I had made the right decision.

Although becoming a Christian was the most positive
thing I'd ever done, it didn't change the way I felt about
myself or stop me from using the coping mechanisms I
thought I needed just to keep going. I was constantly
trying to give up my eating disorder and stop self-harming so I could live a normal, happy, Christian life, but I
had no other methods for dealing with what went on
inside my head. I wanted to be a good Christian but I
couldn't deal with my emotions except through food
and self-harm. My eating habits (which I still hadn't
learned were a disorder – I thought of them as poor self-
discipline) had too strong a hold on me for me to be able
to do anything about them. I read in the Bible that
Christians enjoyed "great joy in the Lord," so I felt guilty
every time I was sad and had to use food or self-harm to
feel better. I felt like a complete failure.

I see-sawed between hating myself for eating and
starving to feel okay, always aware that I was being a bad
Christian. The problem was that although becoming a
Christian had changed my entire outlook, it had very little effect on my "inlook." I thought because all Christians
were saved they must be happy, and my self-esteem sank
even lower because I wasn't. Before becoming a
Christian I had hated myself despite having nothing to
measure myself against. Now I had a yardstick by which
to measure my awfulness, and I could see clearly that I

was somewhere way below the starting point of being a good Christian. I sang up at the front, but I was unable to tell anyone about the battle I was fighting with each urge inside my head. I couldn't admit to anyone that I wasn't all I seemed to be on the outside. The façade I'd built was far more attractive than the weak and disgusting creature I felt I really was.

I had learned a lot about what the Bible says about Jesus loving everyone unconditionally, and because I believed that the Bible was the word of God I knew that it all had to be true. But, at the same time, my self-esteem was so low that I remained convinced that I was a horrible person. I couldn't accept that God could love me. I fully and easily accepted that he loved everyone else, but because I knew I was a bad person I struggled with the idea that I belonged on a planet that God had created for his pleasure. I thought that all I was doing was spoiling his perfect creation; I felt ashamed that Jesus had given his life for someone as awful as me and I knew that I didn't deserve to be a Christian.

My parents were supportive of my becoming a Christian, because they were supportive of everything I did, but they didn't get very involved with that part of my life. They didn't have any idea how depressed I was feeling or how big a problem my eating disorder was becoming. I didn't want them to be worried, and I didn't want to let them down, so I made a concerted effort to avoid them. If I'd been able to talk about some of this with my mother it might have made life easier, but something always stopped me and I kept quiet, feeling like a fraud in the wash of her encouragement, knowing that I was unworthy of all the praise.

❀   ❀   ❀   ❀

I was halfway through writing an English essay in my room one night when I heard Mum call my name.

"Abbie! Can you come downstairs please? We need to talk to you."

I grumbled to myself as I put down my pen – I hated being interrupted when I was working, and I really wanted this essay to be good. I stomped down on each stair to show how disgruntled I was. I found Mum and David sitting on the sofa facing Dad, who was sitting in the rocking chair. My annoyance gave way to apprehension. It looked like an important conversation was about to take place. Mum held out a hand to me, gesturing me to sit down. I perched on the edge of the sofa, wanting to be anywhere but there. Dad took a deep breath.

"I'm an alcoholic."

Those words knocked the breath right out of me. I couldn't have been more surprised if he'd said he was leaving home to be the sultan of some far eastern country. Dad looked at us, as if expecting me or David to say something, but we were both speechless.

Mum filled the silence for us. "I know this is sudden, kids. I've known for quite a while, but we decided you were old enough to understand and realized that for Dad to get better you both had to know. Is there anything you want to ask us?"

I didn't know what to say or how I was supposed to react.

David's voice was accusing: "How long has it been going on? And why all of a sudden did you decide to tell us now?"

Mum looked to Dad. "It's been going on for a while," he said. He cleared his throat. "A long while – about ten years on and off. But it's got worse lately, and I needed to tell you because I appeared in court today and had my license revoked for drunk driving. So we won't be able to drive anywhere for a while. I'm so sorry."

He burst into tears. I didn't know what to do or say.

Dad wiped his eyes with his handkerchief. "I'm going to get help though. I'm going to stop drinking and go to AA, and everything will be better. I promise. It'll be alright kids, don't worry."

David and I stood there awkwardly for a few minutes and mumbled something about how we loved him. I couldn't leave the room fast enough, and I dashed back into my bedroom to the safety of my essay. A couple of minutes later I heard a quiet tapping, and David stuck his head around my door. He came in and sat on my bed.

"So what do you think?" David asked. He made himself comfortable and I kicked his enormous feet off my pillow.

"I have no idea. Did you have any clue what was going on?"

"No, not a one. I mean, I *really* didn't know. It's not even like there were signs – I can't remember ever really seeing him drunk, except sometimes at Morris things. But then it was just because everyone was."

"I know. Ten years? I feel so stupid for never noticing. It's such a big thing, and I was too self-absorbed to notice it." I let the guilt wash over me. How could I have completely missed something so huge? David elbowed me in the ribs.

"Come on, Abs. It's Dad. He's always been a bit melodramatic. He'd make an oil tanker out of a molehill if he could. He's just making a big deal out of it. It'll blow over soon, you'll see." David jumped off the bed and grabbed a couple of my CDs on his way out, leaving the door wide open.

I got up and slammed the door after him – he was so irritating sometimes, and so blasé about things that really mattered. But I had to admit he was usually right, and for the first time I decided to follow his lead. Maybe I could be too melodramatic about things, too. So we all ignored it, respecting the unspoken agreement to treat it as just a small thing.

❀   ❀   ❀   ❀

In all of this I never really knew whether food was my friend or foe. Although I couldn't have articulated at the time what I wanted my eating disorder to achieve, I was looking for something I could trust to stay the same because everything else in my life seemed so complicated and out of control.

Food is, basically, quite simple. You put it in your mouth, you chew it, you digest it, and it keeps you going for a while until you need more. It was an equation that I could understand, and one that I wanted to change. I became obsessed with this idea of body maintenance and fuel. I was determined to live on less than everyone else needed. It wasn't just about losing weight, although the idea that I'd get smaller if I didn't eat was certainly captivating. It was more about trying desperately to control something in my environment. I couldn't control what happened at school or home, or what other people thought of me. I certainly didn't feel that I could control what I was feeling – my emotions were the scariest thing in the world to me, and when they bubbled up from under the surface I never knew how to deal with them. Controlling my intake of food gave me something else to think about. If I could concentrate on what I was eating when, and how much, and what it would do to my body, everything else seemed somehow more manageable.

As I became more and more obsessed with food, everything and everyone else faded into the background of my consciousness. I had friends, but no one with whom I was as intimate as I was with my eating disorder. I put on a personality for everyday life, but behind the façade I swung between wanting desperately to have this disorder and wishing it would go away because it scared me. I had sudden flashes of clarity when I realized that I might not be the one in control, that perhaps the eating disorder had control of me.

Because I worked hard at keeping that distance between myself and everyone else in my life, I don't think anyone suspected what was going on. Certainly no one ever came up to me to ask if I was okay. I had built myself a reputation – I was unapproachable and immersed in my studies and I didn't talk much to anyone. All my friends also worked hard and socialized only occasionally between essays.

Music remained my focus and real love, and also provided some affirmation as I was given leads in the school plays and solos in the choir. Helping with the school campaign to raise money to build a performing arts facility put me in contact with Wendy, an accompanist, and Alice, a singer, who both gave me invaluable tips on performance. They imparted just the right combination of encouragement and criticism to enhance my confidence. They appreciated my help in the campaign office and were also concerned about me.

Then a new girl who was a superb singer transferred from another school, and all of a sudden I was no longer first in line for solos or recognition. All the things I had been aspiring to were suddenly out of reach. I had been counting on a singing part in the school play, but with Amy on the scene I didn't get one. I didn't get any solo parts in the choir, either – an aspiration I had had for years. In all of my subjects, and in all the activities I got involved in, there was always someone better. And, at my school, if you weren't the best you weren't recognized at all. Hard work only paid off if it got you to the top.

I wanted to go on to study music, but my exam grades weren't good enough to get me into the universities I chose. Had I had a chance to sit back and take stock, I might have decided to take some time out, to question what I really wanted to do and figure out whether university and music were for me. But, with the pressure of school, I didn't have that opportunity, and after a nightmarish few days I ended up with a place at Durham – a university better and more highly thought of than my original choices.

❀   ❀   ❀   ❀

One Sunday morning before I left for university, a woman with curly hair and a kind and open face came up to me after church.

"You look like you need a hug," she said. "Can I give you one?"

After releasing me from a bear hug, she introduced herself and asked a difficult question. "Why do you need hugging? Why do you look so sad?"

I spent over an hour pouring out my heart to Anne – my difficulties with Dad and my disappointment about not getting the exam results I'd wanted. In Anne I found a kindred spirit, who understood things in the same way and shared many of my quirks and foibles. She became one of the few people in whom I felt I could fully confide. I knew she would never be judgmental about anything I said.

Around this time I also got to know Jayne and Graham and their two daughters as I joined them each Sunday for lunch. They accepted and loved me and eventually promoted me from friend to third daughter. One of the things I loved about being part of their family was that their house was predictable. Because of Dad's drinking, I often spent entire days at my house hiding in my room just to avoid a confrontation with him. At Jayne and Graham's I knew exactly what was acceptable and what wasn't, and there was no up-and-down in the way they treated me. I spent many a happy afternoon curled up in the corner of their dark blue sofa, soaking up the peace and calm that I didn't feel at my own house.

I was able to open up to both Anne and Jayne about the problems I was having with eating. With their encouragement and understanding I began to increase my intake of food, which improved my mood and helped me to start looking forward to things again. I felt more on an even keel than I had for a long time, and I felt ready to go off to university. They both promised to write me lots of letters, and I knew that they would encourage me to write back to them as truthfully as possible. With this new accountability, I was full of hope that life would be different now.

I embraced university as an opportunity to start again and to escape both the past and the situation at home. I would work hard and be happy with being average if I knew I'd done my best. I was under no false pretences – I knew that I would be a very little fish in an enormous pond. I loaded up the car and set off up the road, exhilarated by thoughts of what might lie ahead.

6

I stood rooted to the floor at my first St. Aidan's College social evening, deafened by the noise and paralyzed by fear as my new-found confidence evaporated.

"Hi!" I heard a voice behind me. I turned around to see a wiry, black-haired guy grinning widely. "I'm Ryan. Isn't this a hoot?"

"Yeah," I answered, trying to sound sure of myself. "But," I added honestly, "I'm not really sure what to do here. I never quite know what to say to people I haven't met. Everyone seems so confident."

"Nah, they're not really. They're all asking everyone the same thing – that way they don't have to think of anything interesting to say!"

I looked at him questioningly.

"There are three questions – where are you from, what were your exam results, and what course are you taking. That's all you need to know to get through this evening. Tell you what, I'll go and get us some drinks and you give it a go. What'll it be?"

"Diet Coke, please. I'm Abbie."

"Nice to meet you, Abbie. I'll be back in a minute," he smiled reassuringly.

I started to circumnavigate the room, asking the same three questions of everyone I saw. By the time I got back to where Ryan was standing with the drinks, I was flushed but exhilarated.

"It worked!"

"And was it fun?" Ryan asked, still smiling.

"It was, actually. I just have to figure out what to do with the rest of my week now. What else is going on?"

Ryan listed off the various parties and bar crawls planned to introduce new students to university life.

"I'm not really a drinker," I said. "Isn't there anything that isn't purely beer based?"

"Well, I'll be at a Christian Union meeting tomorrow. Free coffee and doughnuts, if you're interested." He looked doubtful, as if this offer could lose him a new friend.

"I'd love to. Just tell me where and when, and I'll be there."

Ryan grinned, and we planned when and where we'd meet. On my way back to my new room I gave a little skip – I had my first friend.

The next day, at the first Christian Union social, I realized that I was going to enjoy university. I was in a room full of like-minded people who were all friendly and welcoming. I eagerly signed up for the retreat that was planned for the following month, where the whole group would go away to a youth hostel for a weekend of study, prayer, worship and getting to know one another.

I settled in at college as if I'd been there all my life. I joined some different music and charity groups and made some good friends with whom I'd stay up until all hours, discussing the state of the universe and everything in it. Ryan remained my closest friend. As well as both being Christians we had a lot in common and, while everyone else seemed to be out looking for Mr. or Miss Right, Ryan and I were quite happy staying in my room drinking tea. Ryan had a girlfriend at a different university, and I was completely uninterested in romance, so we spent many easy hours together. Despite all this, however, I just couldn't find it in myself to feel happy and contented.

"It's not that there's anything wrong," I told Jayne on the phone. "There isn't. Everything's fantastic – I love Durham, I love college, and I love studying music. Everything about being a student suits me perfectly. So why do I feel like this?"

Jayne thought for a second. "Maybe you're just expecting too much," she said. "You've always been a perfectionist – if life isn't absolutely wonderful you think you must have done something wrong. Maybe it's just that you're taking time to settle in. I know you didn't like living at home very much, but it's still traumatic to make such a huge change."

"I just feel like I should be making the most of every opportunity, and I can't do that with the way I'm feeling. I wanted to get away from everything I used to struggle with, but it's all still there." I sighed.

"Of course it is – you never actually dealt with the issues that caused your eating disorder. But that doesn't mean that your whole time at university is a failure. If anything, it's an opportunity to find out all the things you have to deal with and take the time to work things through. Maybe you could even find the university counselling office – I'm sure there must be one."

I was silent for a moment. I had never liked the idea of counselling. "The problem is," I explained, "I don't know what I'd say. I know I'm feeling bad, but I don't know why. It's the same as always. I just don't know what's wrong with me."

❀   ❀   ❀   ❀

When the retreat weekend finally arrived we all squeezed into a decrepit bus and headed out for a tiny youth hostel in the middle of nowhere. We studied Ephesians, which was wonderful, and I loved being with like-minded people for a whole weekend.

Still, I couldn't escape these niggling feelings of depression. I was determined to enjoy the weekend, but I couldn't escape from this suffocating sadness. On the last morning, during a time of worship, I felt completely crushed by despair. I tried desperately not to cry. Why was everyone around me so animated and on fire for God when I felt so low? I knew what they were singing about, but I wanted my faith to make my everyday life more bearable. It didn't seem fair that everyone else was living this fulfilled life when I was struggling just to keep going.

I'd had enough. I decided, for the first time ever, to have it out with God. "It's not fair!" I silently shouted at him. "Why don't you make anything better? Why can't I be like everyone else? I'm sick of feeling like this – it's not what your word said I'd feel. I want to be full of joy because I'm a Christian, but right now I don't even know if I want to believe anymore. I want to love you, but I don't even like you right now. What are you doing with my life? I just don't get it! I can't take it anymore!"

I waited for God to strike me down, or whatever he did to dissenters like me. Suddenly I was crying, but I had no idea why. It was such a relief. As I cried, something was released – it was like a breath of fresh air entered my vacuum-packed mind and finally everything was free to move around again. I could almost hear God saying, "It's okay, you're okay as you are. You're my child and I love you. Even if you hate me, you're still beautiful and acceptable."

Before long I was sobbing and crumpled in a heap in the floor. I have no idea how long I knelt and wept, but eventually I was smiling and singing. I sang at the top of my voice and spent the rest of the day with a grin on my face. Everyone I talked to noticed that something was different.

After experiencing God's love so tangibly, I felt much more able to relax and face the days. The worry and the tension had gone. The pressure of being me and having something elusive I had to live up to eased a little as I felt accepted by God for who I was. I enjoyed the rest of that term more than any other time in my life.

Although the retreat had a profound effect on the way I lived at university, I wasn't sure what it would be like at home, where I was the only Christian in my family. Once I got home for Christmas break, I felt all the tension come flooding back. I didn't know how to behave, and I started worrying again about everything I did. The situation with Dad's drinking had deteriorated and, although I had always loved Christmas, I couldn't wait to get back to college in January. I found it easier to relax again then, but never again did I feel the same freedom from pressure I'd experienced in the weeks following the retreat.

❀　　　❀　　　❀　　　❀

I heard Jack whooping with laughter before I ever met him. I was on my way to the pay phone and saw him jumping up and down.

"What's with you?" I asked him.

"My roommate's in the phone booth," he said, hysterical with laughter. I had no idea why that was so funny until I peered around the corner to see the phone booth – it was plastered with tape and shaking as Jack's roommate pounded the door that refused to open

"What have you done?" I laughed, amazed that anyone would do something so crazy.

"He was annoying me by practicing fencing moves in the room when I was trying to work, so I decided to get rid of him for a while. Great idea, huh?"

"Sounds good to me! I guess I'll have to use the other phone though." I turned around to leave.

"Hey!" he shouted after me. I turned around. "You going to the bar later?" I thought about it for a millisecond.

"Maybe," I smiled, knowing there'd be no stopping me now.

"Maybe I'll see you there then." He turned his attention back to the phone booth and his roommate, and I smiled.

Over the next few days we spent more and more time together. We made our relationship official at a fairy tale ball – I was dressed as Peter Pan, he was Tinkerbell. Jack encouraged me to have fun and fought against my over-serious side. He stopped me from doing lots of things I thought were necessary in order to do things that were fun, and I began to realize that I could have fun and didn't have to work constantly.

Jack awoke all sorts of feelings in me. He loved me in such an active way – always complimenting me and giving me things to let me know how much he valued me. Being with him did wonders for my self-esteem. Although I was still experiencing depression most of the time, I also felt nurtured and cared for and was completely comfortable in Jack's company. We spent most evenings together, either socializing or curled up in my room talking about anything and everything. The popular crowd recognized us as a pair, and I loved how that made me feel. We spent the Easter holiday together – a week with my parents and then a week with his family.

But after Easter, despite my relationship with Jack, I began to find life in general more and more difficult again. I felt isolated and depressed, and I didn't know why it had happened or how to pull myself out of it. The world became flat and grey. Although my eating patterns had been better since starting university, I began to alternate between skipping meals and throwing up after eating so that no one would guess what was going on. I finally plucked up the courage to go to my doctor. She was very understanding, completely non-judgmental, and said there was no reason I should carry on that way. She gave me a prescription for Prozac, which was supposed to help my brain get back in balance.

The Prozac didn't have much effect. I felt the load lighten a little, but it was more the result of Dr. Wardle's acceptance than the pills. The issues that were responsible for what I was feeling were still there, and, despite the medication, I couldn't shake them. I didn't feel I had a right to be unhappy, so rather than sharing the burden with Jack and my other friends I pretended that everything was okay. If I'd told them how depressed I was it might have been easier to break the habits, but I couldn't bring myself to ask for their support.

Eventually I told Jack that I was taking antidepressants. He couldn't understand how they worked, why they worked, or why a Christian would need them. He was kind, but he thought I was making a big deal about nothing. So I tried to make it nothing by keeping my feelings locked up behind my happy student façade.

I couldn't figure out what was wrong with me. When I was with people, I wanted to be alone. When I was alone, I was desperate for company. Nothing was right and everything was wrong, but I didn't know why. I lived my pain by proxy, listening to music about teenage angst grown old and reading books about death and suicide and the poetry of Sylvia Plath and Anne Sexton. I couldn't pin down my own pain, so I stole the pain of others, often quoting huge chunks of things when I couldn't verbalize anything myself. Friends kept asking me what was wrong, and I could only tell them the truth – nothing. I couldn't put my finger on why I felt so out of place. I wanted an explanation, some deep-seated tragedy that accounted for my dissatisfaction, but there was nothing. I could see the puzzle of it – nothing was wrong, but I certainly wasn't right.

That summer evening I sat on the window ledge of my upstairs room, feet on my desk, blowing smoke out the window. I was a novice smoker and wasn't even inhaling – cigarettes were more about giving me something to do with my hands than anything else. The cigarettes weren't having much effect – I needed something more tangible than smoke. Once the idea of cutting came into my mind, I couldn't dismiss it.

I found an old Bic razor in the cupboard under my sink. It was quite difficult to liberate the blade from the ugly pink plastic, and once I got it out I was surprised by how small and uncontrollably bendy it was. Still, I made the best of it and went ahead as planned. I told my hand what to do, but, with a mind of its own, it stopped within a hair's breadth of the skin on my upper arm, coming to rest only lightly with the cool sensation of metal on skin. After three false starts my hand finally followed through, and, with a sound that I will always recognize, the blade cut slickly through and opened the skin on my arm. In the exquisite pain the world suddenly fell silent. The ringing in my head stopped, and I felt complete relief and utter calm. It was as if the world had stopped moving, and I finally had the chance to catch up. Even at that moment I knew I was hooked. Finally, something worked.

Because I couldn't explain what was wrong, I went on living as if everything was right. Anorexics, or so I thought, were very skinny young girls being force-fed in hospitals. I, on the other hand, was living a relatively normal student life. And as for my odd bouts of self-harm – I didn't fit the psychotic profile of people I imagined had a problem with cutting themselves. I engaged in my bizarre rituals in the depths of the night so no one could see how weird I was. I was so depressed that I had no regular sleep pattern – and I wasn't eating enough to sleep anyway. I wandered around the campus in the early hours of the morning. I sat for hours in the computer room, where I discovered chat rooms, and chatted to depressed Americans who helped me to open up. These faceless people knew more about me than most of my friends. Venting at night meant I could function during the day.

When a girl called Ellen stood up during a Christian Union meeting and talked about how difficult she had found her first year of college because she was struggling with anorexia, I was fascinated. I had never heard anyone be this open about having an eating disorder. I didn't realize, either, that it could get better. When I asked to talk with her she took me to her room, and I shared some of the things I'd been struggling with. We formed a one-way friendship – she listened patiently as I talked about myself for stretches at a time and helped me sort through some of the things I was feeling. As a Christian, she had some grasp of the dichotomy I felt between my faith and my depression, and she prayed that I would have the courage to find help and eventually be able to say I was free, just like she was.

But I couldn't focus on praying these things with her. I went on locking up my struggles with a combination of starving and cutting. She and Jack tried to encourage me to face my fears, and they sat with me in the dining hall while I limped through meals. Their love and care kept me afloat a little while longer, but I wasn't willing to let God work in me – I didn't want him to take my coping mechanisms away. I couldn't trust him to help me feel better – I only wanted to do things my way.

7

The summer at home loomed before me – coping with my dad's drinking, pretending to be okay, missing friends. And it lived up to expectations, but I had so little energy I couldn't even get myself to care very much. Eating with my family forced my diet into some semblance of normal again, and I stopped cutting in case they found out. I walked a lot and drove a lot and sat a lot with my thoughts, such as they were. I also broke up with Jack.

We saw quite a lot of each other that summer but, once I realized that I didn't want to be with him forever, I found it almost impossible to enjoy his company. Instead of seeing that we just weren't right for each other, I decided there was something wrong with me for not loving him enough. After all, everyone said we were perfect together. My feelings of relief when our relationship finally ended quickly turned to self-loathing. I knew I was a horrible person for having dumped him, and an even worse one because I didn't feel badly about it. I castigated myself constantly and had no trouble convincing myself that I would never be worthy enough for someone to fall in love with and marry. After a summer of giving myself these little lectures, leaving home and going back to Durham was the last thing I wanted to do. I didn't want to see Jack or anyone who might think I'd let him down. But I was very good at hiding my feelings.

So I went back and, for a few weeks, I managed to be everything I wanted people to think I was.

❋   ❋   ❋   ❋

Once I had meticulously arranged my new room in the four-bedroom house we had rented for the year, I began to think everything might be alright after all. My housemates were Ryan and two third-year students – Ali, a chemist, and Mark, a mathematician. It was all very balanced – two guys, two girls; two second-year students and two third-year students; two scientists and two artists. It was to be the only balance in my life that year.

From the outside looking in, the school year started amazingly well. Anxious to deny that anything was wrong, I gave everything 110 per cent. Instead of just reviewing and filing my lecture notes, I methodically recopied them all and color-coded them, trying to be the most conscientious student possible. Instead of taking time out for myself and getting proper rest, I would spend hours at friends' houses, listening to their problems, trying to be the best friend possible. I led Bible studies and spent all my money on Bibles and other Christian books for acquaintances who showed the slightest interest in the gospel, trying to be the best Christian possible. I convinced everyone that I was fine – and not right on the edge of spiraling out of control. I almost managed to convince myself.

I was so busy for those first few weeks that eating slid right off my priority list. One day I got up early for a class, put my trousers on, and noticed that I had run out of holes on my belt. I found this somewhat amusing, but in no way worrying, and decided that I'd skip class and go down to the pharmacy to weigh myself. It then occurred to me that I might weigh less when I got there if I walked down. Upon discovering that I had lost twelve pounds since the last time I'd weighed myself, a small wondering popped into my head: "If I don't eat tonight, will I weigh even less tomorrow?"

So curious was I to know whether I could lose more, it didn't really occur to me that this might be a bad idea. I gave up everything but apples and chewing gum and slipped quite comfortably back into the cycle of superiority.

I was soon on a major anorexic high – the control over my body that I gained by not eating gave me the power to do or be anything I wanted. I achieved so much in those first few weeks of starvation and signed up for all sorts of things I had never even thought of doing before. Despite not giving my body fuel, I had more energy than ever. I became addicted to this new Abbie, and I would have done anything to keep her. I started to push at the boundaries of what I allowed myself to do, taking risks and living more recklessly than I ever had before. I went on bar crawls, drinking all night and stumbling home in the early hours, or attended parties and woke up on someone's floor with no memory of the previous night.

One night, because I didn't want to stay home alone, I went to a dance. I jumped up and down to the beat of the cheesy disco music with gusto, thinking that perhaps if I got tired I would sleep well and feel less lonely. I wanted someone to come along and make me feel better. I wanted to feel something – even if only for a short time.

I was standing next to a guy commonly known as Big Ben, who was six foot seven to my measly five foot small. He had flirted with me over the last couple of weeks and seemed like as good a person as any to counteract my loneliness, so I launched myself at him on the dance floor. Noticing my presence around his knees, he began to dance closer, eventually drawing my body close enough to his that I could feel his breath on the top of my head. As his hands ran down my back I found a sensation that took away the desolation, and I allowed him to pick me up and sit me on top of the cigarette machine so that our mouths were level. As he leaned in to kiss me I forgot about how bad I felt, and I kissed him back.

A couple of hours later we took a break. I jogged down the corridor to the bathroom, looking forward to getting back to the darkness and comfort of the common room and Big Ben's arms.

I spotted Ryan in the lobby. He walked towards me, looking upset.

"You okay, Ry?" I asked, out of breath.

"I want you to remember something," he said to me, disappointment clouding his face. "You need to remember the Truth."

He walked away before I could answer, and I stood rooted to the spot. What Ryan said hit me square in the chest. This is not what God would want me to be doing.

I took my cigarette packet from under the strap of my lavender vest top, lit up and left. What Ryan said had such an impact that I completely forgot about Ben. I didn't say goodbye or go back for my jacket. I walked all the way home in a daze. I hardly felt the cold, just the volcano inside my head.

By bringing Christ into the wrong half of my world, Ryan laid the straw on the camel's back of all my worries that led to my eventual disintegration. Until that evening I had been able to maintain a double life – model Christian student by day, drunken rebel student by night. The world saw that I was having a whale of a time, when, behind my different masks for day and night, I was falling apart.

In order to keep everything from falling apart I had to do everything more, trying desperately to keep up the charade that I was fine. I put myself on a liquid-only diet, upped my gym visits to twice a day instead of once and started taking laxatives to keep everything moving out of my body as quickly as possible. After a few weeks of this it became obvious that my complete high was a temporary situation, and I came drifting back down to earth, too depressed to care where I landed. Not even not eating could control my feelings of despair any longer. I existed day-to-day, calorie-to-calorie, pausing only to concentrate on keeping moving.

❀   ❀   ❀   ❀

I woke up and glanced at my clock. It was just after five o'clock in the morning, and I felt funny. I was used to waking up early and feeling the laxatives working, but this was different. The ceiling swam before my eyes as the bed slowly rocked and turned beneath me. The idea that I might be sick crossed my mind, and with that thought my stomach churned. I stumbled down the stairs and into the bathroom. I couldn't feel my hands, and my vision was obscured by brightly dancing dots of red and green and purple and yellow. Then the world turned black.

When I came to I was on the floor. I had no idea how long I had been out of it. I clawed my way to standing, splashed my face with cold water and looked in the mirror. I didn't recognize the person gazing vacantly back at me. Her face was gaunt, and her exhausted eyes struggled to open above the black rings. Her lips were chapped and pale, and her was hair pasted to her fore-head like wallpaper.

Something felt wrong. I had no idea if I was hot or cold, or whether I actually felt ill. I touched my lips and felt nothing, and then suddenly I realized that I couldn't feel my feet on the floor. A hollow ringing resounded in my ears and I found myself wondering who and where I was. I was entombed by indecipherable echoes and too far away from reality to reach for it. Whose was this body I saw hanging below me? I extended unsteady hands to brace myself on either side of the mirror and leaned. I needed to feel something solid.

Suddenly there was a loud crack, and I jumped back to life. I could feel my body again – my feet were back in my slippers and my eyes in my head. I looked down and saw a piece of broken mirror in each hand, reflecting back a distorted vision of someone who looked like me. "Yes," I thought, "that's what I felt like".

As I walked back along the landing to my room, still holding the mirror, Ryan gave a shout from his doorway.

"Abbie! What happened?"

I looked down and saw blood falling from my fingers and noticed a gash up the side of my palm onto my wrist.

Two and two suddenly made fifteen as I understood why I had come back into the land of the living when the mirror broke. I was back in the cycle of self-harm – this time for good. Any time I felt myself floating away from reality I cut myself in places much less noticeable than my hand, but just as effective. I began to recognize the hollow sounds and feelings of spacing out – a state I later learned to call dissociation – and nipped them in the bud with a small slip of a razor blade.

❀   ❀   ❀   ❀

In the space of a few days it began to be obvious on the outside as well as the inside that I wasn't coping with life. My concentration dwindled even further and I stopped doing any work. I started skipping lectures, which I'd never done before. I stopped being my usual, obsessively tidy self, and old cups and dirty clothes piled high around me. I couldn't be bothered to care about anything or anyone. I spent hour after hour on my bed, staring at the wall. I only moved to go down to the college every night.

Although I was as low as I had ever been, I still managed to hide it from my parents. On the phone I felt a million miles away from every conversation and every sentence I spoke, and yet I somehow succeeded in keeping them blissfully unaware of how depressed I was. I didn't want them to worry about me and I also knew that, even if I had wanted to tell them, I wouldn't have been able to find the words. My feelings were so dulled that nothing affected me – positive or negative.

As I was driving down to college one night, I became conscious of a bright light in my rearview mirror. The driver behind me had his high-beam headlights on, and I was struggling to see what was ahead. I flicked my fog lights on and off, thinking that the driver had his high-beams on by mistake.

The light intensified as the car behind got closer, until his bumper was nearly touching mine. I didn't know what to do – the driver was obviously feeling hostile and not taking any hints from me to back off. I felt a jolt as our bumpers kissed, and I gripped the steering wheel with hands so tense I could hardly feel them.

Suddenly all was dark as the other car passed by me, and I relaxed a little, thinking it was over. I was completely taken aback when the other car, now in front of me, did a 180-degree turn in the road ahead and started towards me at breakneck speed. I thought my time had come and might even have closed my eyes against the glare as I slid helplessly towards a head-on collision.

Remarkably, the car didn't hit me. It swerved at the last minute and drove around me, five young blokes laughing as they passed. I didn't know what to do, but stopping seemed like a bad idea, so I continued on to college, shaking uncontrollably.

I parked badly and stumbled to Ellen's room where I curled up in a corner, shivering with cold, unable to give her a cohesive explanation. With a quilt around me, a heater in front of me and two cups of tea inside me, I was finally able to tell Ellen and her best friend what happened. Between us we came up with as much information as possible for the police – which wasn't much. Ellen's friend had cigarettes, and as I smoked I calmed down a little. I spent the rest of the evening there. They asked about what was happening in my life and encouraged me to talk about how I was feeling.

Eventually, Ellen sat forward and took my hands. "Abbie, you're going to have to eat something." Her eyes looked straight into me, and I knew that she cared. I didn't know what to say.

"You look ill, Abbie. You've lost too much weight, and every time I see you I'm worried that you're going to fall over. You need to get some help."

I looked away. In some remote corner of my mind I knew that she was right. I had to do something. So I agreed to let her phone the university counselling office the next day. It couldn't do any harm, and I was beginning to acknowledge that I wasn't going to get better on my own.

My counsellor was called Kath, and she was lovely. She let me talk about everything that was upsetting me and asked all the right questions about what I was doing. I saw her every three or four days, and I felt comfortable enough with her to truthfully share what I was doing and feeling.

But despite seeing Kath and continuing with the antidepressants I'd been prescribed the previous term, I just couldn't pull myself out of this depressive lethargy. I didn't go to classes. Each day I sat for hours staring out the window. At night I purposely put myself at risk by walking alone in dodgy areas, hoping that someone else would end it all for me. I didn't eat, I hardly slept, and I rarely interacted with anyone except to smile wanly at conversations I could make no sense of. I was unable to make decisions and wore the same clothes every day for a week.

❀   ❀   ❀   ❀

One day, in Kath's office, I lost the words to talk. I said nothing for about twenty minutes because I had nothing to say.

Kath leaned forward and put a hand on my knee. "I think I need to take you to the doctor. I know you don't want to go, but I don't think we can cope with this on our own. I think your doctor needs to know, and I think you need more help than I can give you."

"Whatever you say." I was hardly surprised – I didn't react to anything these days.

"You mean you'll come with me right now?" Kath seemed surprised that I hadn't refused – the truth was I simply didn't care either way.

We walked to the doctor's office in silence and waited for twenty minutes to see Dr. Wardle. Kath read a magazine and I looked at my fingers.

In Dr. Wardle's office the conversation washed over me. I let Kath do all my talking for me. I couldn't be bothered to make sense of what they were saying, and I was beyond caring what they decided.

"Abbie?" Dr. Wardle broke into my thoughts and I turned and tried to focus on her. "Did you hear any of that?"

I shook my head.

"I think you should go to the hospital."

The word snapped me back. "Hospital? Why?"

"Because you aren't coping. You're suicidal, you aren't eating, and the depression you have means that you aren't able to make decisions for yourself."

I tried to think. "I don't think I want to," I finally said.

Dr. Wardle moved closer to me until her face was right in front of mine.

"Abbie, you need to understand that there isn't a choice here. I don't want to think about what could happen if someone doesn't look after you."

"But . . ." The sentence trailed away. I didn't have anything to follow the but.

Dr. Wardle looked at me and made up her mind. "Okay, here's what we'll do. We'll make another appointment for tomorrow, which gives you a while to think about it. I know you're having a bad day today, and it might not be entirely indicative of what's going on for you right now. But if things are still like this tomorrow, I won't give you the choice. If I think your life is in danger, I will take measures to force you into hospital. Do you understand what I'm saying?"

"I understand," I whispered. "I'll think about it. I'll see you tomorrow."

I stood up and walked out, leaving Kath with Dr. Wardle.

I walked to one of Durham's many bridges and considered it. On the one hand, I could try to live a normal life, like all the other students I saw around the city. But

I felt so far removed from them. I looked the same on the outside, but on the inside I felt as if they were miles away. The things they talked about didn't make sense to me – we were moving on different planes. On the other hand, I could descend into madness and lead a Plath-esque existence, leaving the real world behind. But, as tempting as it was, it didn't just feel like giving up – it felt fake. Claiming to be mad would have been as unreal as trying to be normal.

After half an hour on the bridge talking to myself, trying to figure out if I was mad or not, I realized that I was in no shape to do anything at all. I walked back to the doctor's office with the decision made that I would go into hospital.

❀   ❀   ❀   ❀

As I stood in the hospital corridor waiting for Julia, one of the nurses, to show me around, I wondered again if I was doing the right thing, and then laughed at myself when I realized that I didn't have anything else to do. I decided the hospital wasn't too bad – it was certainly better than the images of antiquated institutions that been waltzing around my head for the previous few hours. I had my own little cubicle, with a lockable cabinet, and there were plenty of places to sit and mull.

The ward was essentially one long corridor. At one end were the non-smoking room (completely deserted except when visitors came) and the smoking room, which was out of bounds to visitors and was always filled with patients and a comforting fog. At the other end of the corridor was the pool room – a big, circular room with a pool table (and, I later discovered, an escape route through an un-alarmed fire exit, should I ever need it).

At the same end of the corridor as the smoking and non-smoking rooms were the single rooms, where patients on one-to-one observations stayed. The further your room was from this end, the less seriously ill you were – and the bigger the room. I was about halfway down in a dorm with three other people.

It all seemed bearable until the evening when I realized, sitting in the dark in the visitor's room, how completely alone I was. I finally had a license to behave as insanely as I felt – I could scream and shout and kick the barriers of my world. But I couldn't do it. I could do nothing but sit, silently and still. Maybe I wasn't really insane at all. I felt like a fraud.

"Meds!" The sound didn't register. "Meds!"

About five minutes later, a portly nurse marched into the room and snapped on the light. "Meds!" she shouted again.

"Huh?" I squinted up at her.

"You're supposed to be taking your meds. Anti-depressants and sedatives. They were prescribed earlier." She thrust a glass of water under my nose and held out a tiny cup with a rainbow of pills scattered in the bottom. I reached out and took them.

"Sorry, I didn't know," I whispered. She watched me swallow and then gestured for me to open my mouth so she could check I'd really taken them.

"I don't do this for fun, you know," she muttered under her breath as she rolled the squeaking drugs trolley back down the ward. I stood motionless, watching her leave. I wondered what fun she thought I was having.

About ten minutes later, I noticed that I wasn't able to focus on anything. My head felt far too heavy for my body and my feet didn't move in time with one another. As I stumbled along the ward towards my bed, it occurred to me that I'd never taken sleeping tablets before, and these seemed to be strong. As I fell into bed I had one last thought before slipping into oblivion.

"Tomorrow has to be better."

8

After a few days I began to understand – and even appreciate – the finely-tuned hospital routine. I felt so conspicuous, and I wanted to avoid people seeing me at all costs. I didn't feel I deserved to take up any space. I curled up into as tight a ball as possible while sitting on chairs in the TV room and hugged the wall when walking along the corridors. I didn't talk to anyone at all for three days, bar the odd thank you, and I avoided places where people were. But however small I tried to make myself, it was never small enough. I wanted to be without body, some kind of ethereal being that no one could touch.

But eventually I realized that I would have to treat the hospital as my real world now, and I plucked up the courage to venture into the smoking room, where I got to know a few people. There was Bob, the gay alcoholic, who was very softly spoken and took it upon himself to look after me, and Mary, who wore pearls everyday. No one ever really knew what was wrong with Mary. She had been there for as long as anyone could remember and treated the place more like a hotel than a hospital. She was one of the privileged few who was allowed a single room without observation, and, besides being completely barmy, she was one of the most mentally healthy people there – including the staff.

Then there was Nina, another student, who was an anorexic, self-harming borderline patient. We found we

had lots of things in common and quickly became part-
ners in crime. She had been in and out of hospital for
years and she taught me the ropes. She taught me when
you could cut and not be discovered, and she discipled
me in the art of throwing away food unnoticed. Very
few relationships in mental health units are healthy
ones, and this psych ward was no exception. Nina's cur-
rent stint at this hospital was the result of a suicide
attempt (thwarted by a newfound fear of heights) on a
bridge over a major highway. As the police hauled her
into hospital she was kicking and screaming and
demanding her rights, much to the amusement of those
already there.

Nina and I spent hours sitting on the floor in the corridor, as close to the nurses' office as we dared. Because
the office was near the main ward entrance we weren't
allowed anywhere near it on pain of death. During a
shift change you could be escaping or dying or both, and
they still made you wait. The door was always shut, pre-
sumably because that's where they kept the drugs. The
nurse's room was another matter. Although we weren't
allowed in, the door was usually open, and we could
hover and chat if they were in a good mood. We could
also sneak up and listen to their conversations – I once
discovered all sorts of things I didn't know about my
treatment plan. Nina and I would make ourselves comfortable near the door and smell their lunch, and Nina
would talk about how good we were for not eating. I
didn't really do much talking around Nina – she seemed
too confident, and I didn't really know what to say to
her. I felt like a novice in her presence, and she made me
feel abnormal for wanting to get out of my eating disorder.

❀　　　❀　　　❀　　　❀

About ten days after going into the hospital, I finally got up enough courage to phone my mother. She sped straight up to Durham with my dad to make things better.

I sat by the window in the smoking room and watched my parents walking up the hill from the station. I had been looking out for them all morning, dreading their arrival. They looked fraught and were deep in discussion – I was relieved I couldn't hear what they were talking about. I decided to make myself scarce – I wanted to be able to go and find them rather than having them find me.

A few minutes later, I slunk down the left-hand wall of the corridor, refusing to call out until I got close.

"Hi."

Mum reached out to hug me before she said anything. She gathered me up in her arms, but I couldn't respond. I stood limply, arms by my sides, waiting for the conversation I didn't want to have.

"Why didn't you tell us? We didn't know!" she said.

I shrugged. I didn't really know what to say. We stood awkwardly as I tried not to look at mum, who was trying not to cry. Eventually Julia appeared and ushered us into the visitor's room. I curled up in one of the armchairs, avoiding eye contact with Mum and Dad, who'd chosen the sofa. Julia sat in the corner, distancing herself from the conversation. For once, Dad let Mum do all the talking.

"Why didn't you tell us?" she asked again.

"I didn't want to worry you. You have too much going on as it is." I looked over at Dad, who was staring into space. I wondered whether Mum had told him to stay quiet, or whether he really didn't have a grasp of what was going on. Mum launched into a list of all the things that could possibly have gone wrong, like working too hard, partying too hard, trying to help everyone else too much and be all things to all people. I let her go through her list. I knew she couldn't understand what was really going on. I didn't know myself.

"Come home with us. I'll be able to look after you and make sure you get well," there was a pleading edge to her voice.

I knew that Mum just wanted to get me where she could see me, to build me up and get me healthy.

She turned to Julia. "We will be able to take her home, won't we?"

Julia looked at her and then at me. She didn't say a word. I watched Mum's face as the realization dawned that there was more going on than she knew about, and her despondence made me ache – the last thing I had wanted was for her to be this hurt. That's why I hadn't told her what was going on in the first place.

"Abbie needs to stay here for the time being," Julia answered softly.

I was so glad she hadn't said any more. We all slumped in our chairs – there was nothing else to say.

Trying to make the best of the fact that they were going home without me, Mum and Dad did their best to make the weekend as pleasant as possible. We went for walks around Durham, drank endless cups of tea and filled many hours with small talk. On Sunday afternoon I waved goodbye with relief.

After they left, I sat at the far end of the corridor, as far away from other people as possible. I leaned back against the cold wall and thought about how disappointed my parents had been and how little I'd been able to tell them of what was going on in my head. Of course they were shocked and puzzled – I'd spent years working hard to hide my anxieties from them. It was as if I was looking at myself from the outside, wondering why the reality didn't match the picture I'd created. How could it have come to this? But here I was, nineteen years old, with the whole world open before me, causing myself physical pain in order to detract from the utter desolation that lay just beyond sensation. I could sense the guilt, disappointment, anger and fear from the weekend threatening to spill out. I couldn't cope with the gravity of these feelings, and I dug my nails into my arms to try and stop them from escaping, but it didn't seem to be doing any good. I began to panic and threw my head back against the wall. I heard the thud of my skull against painted plaster and I relaxed slightly, the feelings temporarily abated. I'd make it to tomorrow, even if tomorrow was just another day to get through.

Once I'd settled in, the staff decided that eating more healthily would be the first goal of my treatment plan. I wasn't dying from malnutrition but "a bit on the thin side." The plan was comprehensive. I had to have breakfast, but I could eat it in my room. I had to eat two meals in the dining area a day, but only one could be salad. They tried to make it as easy as possible and ordered me a pint of skimmed milk every other day to have with my low-fat, low-calorie, low-taste cereal, but they didn't account for how deceptive I could be. They never got around to telling the kitchen staff what I was allowed, so I thwarted the plan each mealtime. In the first three days, I lost five pounds.

The whip was cracked. A nurse was assigned to watch me during mealtimes to make sure that I ate a full cooked meal, including a dessert. Snacks also magically appeared through the day, which, depending on the nurse, varied from apples to cookies.

"It's a good plan, Abbie, I promise," Julia would say as she sat with me, watching every swallow. "It'll get easier, you'll see."

But it didn't. Controlling my food intake was the only way I knew to deal with each day and its emotions. Although I wasn't coping very well in general before I'd been admitted to the hospital, I'd had very clear boundaries around everything. I knew exactly how much food I was eating, how many laxatives I was taking and how much exercise I was doing, and I was therefore managing to keep a tight rein on my emotions. By controlling my body I could contain the chaos. As unhealthy a coping mechanism as it was, it had its uses and meant that I could function. Without it, I wasn't sure I could cope. Nothing seemed certain anymore. The chaos was threatening, and I needed another way to keep it under lock and key. And so I found the security of the razor blade.

Although I had newly discovered its effectiveness, self-harming was not, at this point, a way of life. I hadn't ever been serious about causing myself damage, I had just used it to avoid dissociating – spacing out to the extent I couldn't make sense of anything. Up until this point, all my efforts had been focused on food. Once the hospital staff took away my control of what went into me with their prescribed menus, force-feeding and constant watching, I began to panic. My grasp of reality began to slip away, and I didn't know what was wrong. Nothing felt right. Now that I couldn't think about what to eat when, how much would make me fat, how little I could get away with, how many calories were hidden in things, what I looked like, or what people would think when they saw me eating, there seemed to be nothing left. Once my diet became public domain, my relationship with food went from being a monogamous affair to an unreliable acquaintance – sometimes a good pal, others a sworn enemy. So I found another friend, and for a while we were as close as could be.

Cutting was a back-up – my safety measure. I had smuggled razor blades into the hospital in my purse. Since that day I'd spaced out in the house, I'd been petrified of the same thing happening again, so I'd started taking razor blades everywhere with me, just in case. Once I had overcome the initial fear of being discovered and had started cutting, it was very hard to stop. Before going to the hospital I hadn't taken cutting seriously at all. It took time in a psych ward to turn me into a pro.

I would get into such a state that I wouldn't know what to do with myself, or what might happen next. The pressure built up inside me until I lost contact with the world outside, and got trapped inside my head. Feelings of anger and frustration made me panic – I was petrified that someone might see what I was really like, that I wasn't the quiet, sweet girl they all thought I was. So I vented these feelings through harming myself. It didn't make me feel better about myself, but it grounded me again. The feelings somehow escaped in the process of cutting, and I felt safe.

Soon I was cutting on an almost daily basis, building up a library of scars on my chest and stomach. The steri-strips were like a security blanket and the constant soreness comforted me, letting me know I was still alive and able to feel something. As the cutting got worse, the staff often found out – it's hard to wash blood out of shirts unnoticed when you share a ward with 20 other people. Sometimes I'd cut badly enough that I couldn't sort out my injuries by myself, and I would have to go and find Julia or another nurse to help me clean up. Every time they knew I'd cut myself they would confiscate the blades and ask if I had any more. I always said no, but I was never without a supply hidden in my drawer ready for next time. Every time they tried to reach out to help me, I turned my back – cutting was something I did for myself, and I didn't want anyone else infringing on it.

I hoped that cutting would enable me to eat normally and so placate the nurses. But as those who were caring for me crossed and tried to reshape the very strict boundaries I had set up around food and my body, my eating became chaotic in an entirely new way. I became as desperate to get hold of food as I had once been to avoid it. I stole food from anywhere I could get it – other patients' lockers, food trays, kitchen cupboards. I secretly ate anything I could get my hands on, just to feel like I was the one controlling my diet.

❀ ❀ ❀ ❀

"I don't think we should be kept locked up in here like prisoners. We need something beyond than these four walls. Just because we're in a loony bin doesn't mean we don't have rights." Nina was waxing lyrical about the limits of being in the hospital and stirring up mutiny among the patients.

"It's not a loony bin, Nina. It's a mental health ward where people come to get better." Julia and the other nurses had heard it all before.

"She's right though," Bob piped up from his corner, cigarette hanging from his mouth. "We need some fresh air, some stimulation. It's more depressing in here than it is in the real world. How do you expect anyone to get better?"

Other patients began chipping in with their ideas about our rights. I kept quiet and Mary stared blankly out the window.

Julia held up her hands in a call for quiet. "Okay, people! If we go on a planned walk every few days will that make things better?"

There was an unspoken discussion as the patients looked at each other.

"It'll do for now," Nina said, leaning back in her chair as if her job was done.

The first walk was planned for after breakfast the next morning. I hadn't intended to go, but Nina persuaded me that I should.

"It'll be a laugh," she said. "They'll never let you go out on your own if you don't start coming on the group things."

That seemed to make sense, so I bundled up against the Durham frost and walked down the hill, listening to Nina chatter and breathing in the crisp air. As we approached the shopping area I pulled my hat down and scarf up, determined not to be recognized by anyone I knew. I followed the crowd as they pleaded to go into the different shops.

As we were walking up the main street, a pharmacy caught my eye and planted an idea in my head. I caught Matt, one of the young student nurses, by the sleeve.

"I need to go into the pharmacy. Can I go on my own? I need tampons, and I don't want the others to know." He smiled down at me from his lofty six feet.

"I don't see why not. I'll stand outside and wait. Be quick, okay?"

I scuttled in and scanned the shelves. Within two minutes I was out, clutching a small bag of laxatives and razor blades.

Matt smiled. "Okay?"

"Fine. Thanks." I jogged down the road after him to catch up with the others, basking in the brilliance of my new scheme.

After a couple of weeks, I was finally allowed out on my own. After behaving so well with the supervised groups, and then with other patients, I was deemed healthy enough to start venturing into the world alone – for a limited amount of time, of course. I eagerly anticipated the afternoon of my first solo trip.

"Are you sure you want to go?" Julia asked. I nodded eagerly. "Do you have everything you need? Have you got some money in case you need to phone us?"

"I'll be fine, really. I'm just going for a walk to be alone with my thoughts. A bit of fresh air will do me good."

Julia wrote my name in her book and held it out for me to sign. "Back in an hour, okay?" She had her stern face on, curly hair framing a frown that I wasn't about to mess with.

"No problem. See you soon."

My heart started beating faster as I strode down the hospital driveway towards my car. I took one last look over my shoulder to make sure I hadn't been spotted and slid behind the driver's seat.

"Come on, car, start," I urged as I turned the ignition. The car spluttered to life and I pulled away. I knew the route like the back of my hand. I was on my way to the grocery store to buy food.

Fifty-five minutes and about three thousand calories later, I walked back into the ward and found Julia.

"I'm back," I gasped, out of breath from the run back upstairs.

"You're early," she said, eying me up and down. "Did you have a nice walk?"

"Lovely, thanks. It was nice to get some fresh air and exercise. I feel all healthy now." I almost skipped back down to my little cubicle, delighted in the secret knowledge that now I had a way to manage whatever the hospital threw at me. All of a sudden, my hospital stay became far more manageable, and my eating disorder veered off in a whole new direction.

After only one trip to the grocery store I was addicted, and I waited anxiously for those two or three days a week when I was allowed out alone. Once I'd started to eat, I couldn't stop – it was too exciting. I went whenever I was allowed out. I ate more and more each time and fooled the nursing staff into thinking I was doing better. While it felt good to have this secret, I couldn't get past feeling disgusted with myself. It felt so sinful to be indulging in something I didn't feel I deserved, and I was ashamed of my need for what seemed to me like ridiculous amounts of food. I had to keep it a secret – I was certain that the shame I felt inside would show on my face.

As the weeks went by I ate more and more each time. I didn't enjoy it – I hated myself for doing it in the first place, and more often than not I ate food that I hated the taste of just to feel suitably punished. And yet I couldn't stop myself. I ate two or three days' worth of calories in one sitting, and the worse my day was (according to my own shuttered view of the world), the more I would eat – just to punish myself. Although I couldn't see it at the time, this was another way of using food to control my emotions. With each grotesque mouthful I was just stuffing my feelings back down again.

Before long I was putting on weight and beginning to panic about my intake. I did lots of exercise in secret – certainly more than was healthy considering the state my body was in. I also started to take laxatives again, but they didn't have the desired effect – physically or emotionally. Making myself sick seemed to be the only way to neutralize what I felt about the bingeing, and eventually I couldn't binge without throwing up. The ritual didn't feel complete without it. Being sick was as important for my emotional serenity as the eating itself, and meant that I could just about face the hospital meals.

After six weeks in the hospital I was getting rather bored. Christmas was coming and I wanted to be at home, not staring at the four vomit-green walls of my cubicle.

I fought the case with my consultant when he came around for his weekly chat. "I'm so much better – I'm eating every day, and I'm not suicidal, and I think I need to be with my family. Being in here is just bringing me down."

He spoke without looking up from his notes. "But you're not well yet, Abigail. What makes you think you could cope with leaving us?"

I hated it when he used my full name – it made me feel like a naughty schoolgirl. I had told him numerous times that I was called Abbie, but he never seemed to take it on board.

"I don't think this is a healthy place for me to be," I began. "Nina keeps telling me what I should be doing, which isn't helping, and I want to go back to real life. I'm not doing anything here – at least if I'm at home with my parents I can do something. I know I'm not better yet, but I want to be. Being here has helped, but it can't get me all the way. I'm ready to start making my own decisions," I lied with my best smile, the same smile that had usually gotten me what I wanted when I was a child.

He flicked back through the pages of my file. "It does look like things are getting better. You've managed to put and keep some weight on, and you're injuring yourself less. Do you really feel like you're ready?"

I hoped he couldn't see the desperation in my eyes. "I really do. I don't think there's anything else I can achieve while I'm stuck in here."

"Well, it's not something I would normally suggest, but as you signed yourself in you have the right to sign yourself out. At least if you're at home with your parents I know you'll be supported. When do you want to leave?"

"I want to be home by Christmas."

"That gives us two weeks. Do you think you'll be ready then?"

"I'm certain of it. I just want to go home." I looked at him pleadingly.

"Alright then, I'll talk to Julia, and we'll sort it out. Have a good day, Abigail – I'll see you next week."

As I left the room, I marveled at how easy it had been to persuade him. If I hadn't managed to hide everything from the nursing team so well, there would be no way I could go home. I was self-harming every day and bingeing every time I went out. I had finally come to the realization that if I behaved in the way I was supposed to, they'd let me out. I threw up three meals a day like a good little girl, and stopped telling them when I'd cut. I was maintaining my weight and not about to throw myself in front of a train – I certainly looked cured. Although I wasn't about to let on, I did wonder how on earth I'd gotten away with everything I'd done and continued to do. What good had all these weeks here done me?

I recalled the conversation I'd had with Dr Wardle six weeks previously. I knew she'd been right about sending me to the hospital, because I had been suicidal at the time, but it was hard to see any other positives. Their main achievement was managing to keep me alive for a few weeks longer, giving me enough time out of reality to work up the fight to keep going. The only other benefit was a medication cocktail that had had an effect.

While I had resisted and rebelled against a lot of the hospital rules, I think I was disappointed. I'd pictured more – counselling sessions, occupational and art therapy, hours in groups comforting, hugging and encouraging other patients. I wanted to figure out why I did what I did and what it was that had turned me into a psycho-lunatic.

I had almost looked forward to all the necessary self-examination. I hated the life I was living, and I was desperate to get out of the cycle I was trapped in. I had had visions of going back to college and saying, "Look at me, I got it sorted, I'm better." But, after spending six weeks sitting in the TV room smoking, the only improvement I saw was in the amount of nicotine I could stomach. I went from smoking a few cigarettes here and there to thirty a day, and so finished my time as an inpatient with a brand-new addiction.

I needed someone to confront me, care for me, love me, take all decisions away from me, and essentially bring me back to life. But, at the same time, I was terrified that I wouldn't be able to deal with life without the coping mechanisms I had in place. I desperately wanted to be better, but bingeing and cutting were the only things that were keeping me going. Although the hospital staff did their best to help me stop damaging my body, they didn't give me any other ways to cope with life. So, every time they tried to intervene, I shrank back, unable to accept their help because I was too scared that they would take away the only methods I had to cope. They didn't know what to do, and neither did I. We were all just treading water, trying to find a workable compromise that would keep me alive.

I spent Christmas at home with my family, sleeping in my own bed and avoiding my own dinner table. I had an outpatient appointment set up for January, and I was given very strict guidelines under which I would be able to stay out of the hospital. I had to stay over 110 pounds and not cut. My consultant didn't come to my outpatient appointment. His assistant asked how I was, to which I gushingly replied that I was doing really well and getting my life back. She didn't examine or weigh me. I weighed 96 pounds and was covered with steri-strips, but I never heard from the hospital again.

9

Once I got home, pretending everything was fine became something of an art form. I was intent on appearing to be as normal as possible – partly because I didn't want to be noticed. I shrank into the background and put on my old familiar coping face. Each day blurred into the next. I didn't want anyone to know what had happened to me – I just wanted to hide from the world.

Of course, I'd been in hospital, so my family knew that things hadn't been right, and it was much harder to pull the wool over their eyes than it had been previously. They tried to act as if everything was fine, as if my hospitalization was just a blip and any problems were now resolved. I certainly pretended that that was the case. However, because I hadn't worked through any of the real issues in the hospital, nothing was any better. The draw to my eating disorder and self-harm was too strong, and most days I succumbed.

With the state things were in at home it was easy to act as if I was fine. While I had been in Durham, Dad's drinking problem had finally forced him to leave his job. So he spent his days at home, supposedly recovering.

For a long time we had blamed Dad's drinking on job-related stress and, although it got pretty bad towards the end of his teaching career, we all thought that once he stopped working he'd be okay. As it turned out, a combination of more time and less responsibility was the last thing he needed. By the time I arrived home he was drinking more than ever, earlier and earlier in the day. His mood swings became more and more extreme, and we never knew where he was or what he might do next. He stormed out of the house after throwing tantrums over the most insignificant things and went straight to the store to buy vodka, which he drank on the way home. When he returned he either lost his temper again, causing monumental arguments, or went straight up to the bedroom, where he passed out for hours. None of us ever knew what was going to happen next, and we tiptoed around in fear of sparking a reaction in him.

When he was at home, David usually bore the brunt of my father's rages. When all four of us were involved, David and Dad generally fought it out while Mum and I stayed on the sidelines, trying to offer peaceful solutions without being drawn in ourselves. The alcohol made him want to hurt people emotionally, which was so unlike the dad I knew when he was sober. Dad always knew which buttons to press, and he managed to find weak spots in every opponent. He railed on David about his school work and shouted at Mum for being unsupportive of him – the weak spot he found for me was my faith.

One evening, I was curled up reading a book when Dad swaggered in. He usually didn't argue with me, but that night something snapped. He grabbed the book out of my hand and read aloud from the blurb on the back.

"Build faith . . . living a Christian life . . . being part of a church . . . What is all this?" he sneered. I wasn't quite sure how to answer. He didn't share my faith, and when he was drunk he was often quite scathing about it.

"It's – it's just a book I borrowed from a friend at church," I stammered. He threw the book against the wall. I jumped and retreated into the corner of the bay window, trying to hide among the curtains. Dad leaned in towards me until his face was close to mine.

"I don't know why you bother." His voice was loud and he chose his words deliberately. "It's not like you can play any part in a church with the state you're in. They probably wish you'd never walked through their doors."

I began to cry. Somehow he knew exactly what I feared most.

"You call yourself a Christian?" he went on. "Why aren't you forgiving me then? I thought Christians were supposed to love and forgive people – you can't be a very good one can you?"

Tears poured down my face, and I tried to avoid his gaze, despite the fact his face was only inches from mine. I refused to respond. I didn't know what to say, and I didn't want to make things worse. Eventually he gave up. He hit the window frame next to my head and walked away.

I slid down until I was crouched on the floor. I heard him storming through the house. His shouting scared me, and I wanted to hate him, but I wasn't sure he was wrong. Forgiving him was the last thing I wanted to do.

❀   ❀   ❀   ❀

We all tried to maintain some semblance of normalcy in the wake of Dad's whirlwind. For the most part, that meant that we all pretended that everything was okay until the next drunken brawl in our living room.

For me, it meant keeping my efforts to self-destruct a secret and pretending that my stint in hospital had sorted me out. My job, as I saw it, was to cause my mother as little worry as possible. That way she could use all her reserves to face the situation with Dad. She knew that I wasn't completely better, but I refused to let her in, and I only talked to Anne and Jayne. I didn't want my mum to see what her daughter had turned into. So I kept up my double life. On the surface I tried to be the ideal, helpful, caring daughter. In my own world I slowly tore myself apart.

❁   ❁   ❁   ❁

Three months after arriving back home I got a job. It probably wasn't the most sensible plan, but I couldn't bear being in the house with my dad all day while Mum was working and David was at school. As a sales assistant in a local bookshop I spent all day lugging piles of books downstairs, breaking from that only to do a stint at the front desk when the back of the shop got too cold. I was constantly exhausted, and a few hours into the day I would start sucking mints to avoid fainting. I tried desperately to keep my mind off the constant pain in my legs and soul.

My eating disorder raged. I weighed myself numerous times a day, just to see if I'd lost any weight. Part of my daily routine was a trip to the pharmacy to use their scales, because I couldn't trust our scales at home. I began to throw up meals that I had at home so they wouldn't have any effect on the next day. Laxatives also beckoned with a dishonest finger, and I was drawn back into an abusive cycle. I increased my dosage relentlessly, until I was back on forty a day.

Every day was the same, and I still have no idea how I pulled myself through each one. I got up each morning as late as I could to still be at work on time. I walked through town in a daze, trying to think straight. I never ate breakfast, but sometimes I had a cup of tea to wake myself up – especially in the winter months, because I woke up frozen to the bone. Nothing really warmed me, but the hot drink helped. Later I switched to hot water – the same jolt to the system, but without the calories.

My lunch hour was nearly always the two to three o'clock slot. I went for a walk and, on the way back, I weighed myself at the pharmacy. The fate of the rest of my day hinged on that event. If I had lost weight, I would be upbeat for the rest of the day and would go home and be able to socialize a bit with my family. If my weight remained the same, I didn't feel the same level of triumph but I could rest vaguely comfortably in the knowledge that I wasn't getting bigger. If I had gained weight, I would sink into deep depression, find it difficult to talk to anyone at all, and spend all evening alone in my room, chatting to people on the internet, reading, or just lying catatonic, unable to figure out what I should do next.

Then I went to sleep, and the whole thing started again. I could see nothing besides the drudgery of it all. I spent many hours contemplating how much I hated what I had become. I felt like a worm crawling through sludge. There were just a few people I felt able to spend any time with, and only Anne and Jayne knew how bad things really were. I couldn't bear the thought of inflicting myself on other people.

Because I was constantly so low and there was no variation, I didn't realize how depressed I actually was. Although I wanted to get better, I didn't think I deserved to be a whole person, living a normal life. I kept a journal filled with a haphazard mix of poetry and prose comprehensible only to myself. Every entry was about food or how much I hated myself – usually both. I wrote about how I felt like a fraud when people liked me and how, if they knew what I was really like, they wouldn't be able to get far enough away. I wrote about food as undeserved indulgence, and a method of showing other people that I knew I was worthless. I wrote about how fat I felt, where on my body I felt fat, how much I hated my body. Every so often, I recorded an episode in which someone had been nice to me or said something good about me, always punctuated by "Do I deserve it? No."

Most of the entries were in the form of a dialogue between two very distinct voices. The pleading voice told me that I wanted food, that I was hungry, and that I could get better from anorexia by eating. And the tyrannical voice answered back, telling me how little I deserved and how utterly worthless I was:

> When I got home I wanted to limit myself to just one piece of bread and marmite, but a piece of melon was just sitting there and I had to have it. I shouldn't have – I didn't need it, and it was selfish to have it when someone else could have done. Now I want another piece of bread and marmite, even though I know I shouldn't. It's so unfair. Why can't I have it? I know I can't, I'm constantly being told I can't. I can't indulge myself or worse things will happen – I'll have to compensate later and be forced to exercise or take laxatives or worse. I just want to be like everyone else so I can eat and be like normal, but to even want to be is selfish when I'm such a horrible person. Why should I have what everyone else has when I really don't deserve it? I just can't and that's all.

By day I was staunchly anorexic and maintained the control over my intake I so desperately craved. But my number-one priority was not worrying my parents or letting them down – particularly Mum, who had enough on her mind. So I ate normal meals in the evening, which led to snacking and grazing for the rest of the night.

Come morning, I would hate myself for all I'd eaten the night before – and so the cycle would begin again.

It wasn't long before the snacking and grazing escalated to the full-fledged binges I had first succumbed to in hospital. Every time my parents went out, which happened a couple of times a week, I binged and purged, using the physical sensations to mask the emotional pain.

As soon as they were gone I went up to my room, shut the door and turned up the music to drown out my thoughts. I lit candles and turned off the lights so I couldn't see how disgusting I was being. Opening the drawer under my bed brought a feeling of exhilaration as I contemplated the selection of food – cakes, bread, crackers and chocolate – that I hoarded for times like these. I wrapped myself in my quilt and sat on the floor in a corner. I ate quickly, trying to fill the gaping hole that never quite disappeared. I ate anything and everything so there wouldn't be enough room inside for all the feelings that were threatening to come up.

The food always ran out, but it didn't matter – the feelings were under control. For a few minutes that were worth fighting for like eternity, I just sat, feeling calm and contented, like everything was finally okay. The storm had calmed, the pressure had been released, the chaos turned to rich silence, and I could cope with the world. I had been desperate for that all day – that feeling that I could manage life for just a short time. But the euphoria – that brief time I could fully relax – was over far too quickly, and the purging had to start.

I began by throwing up everything I could. I spent hours on the bathroom floor, kneeling on magazines to protect the cream carpet, eyes watering, mouth burning, throat bleeding, skinny models staring up at me from the glossy pages. I drank as many pints of water as I could to loosen it up – I'd do anything I thought would help my body to rid itself of the alien inside me. Even when there was nothing left to throw up I knew I wasn't completely empty, because I didn't feel empty. So I took whole boxes of laxatives.

Finally, when it was all over, I fell into bed exhausted and numb. Despite my sore throat, swollen eyes and aching stomach, I felt more relieved than at any other time during the day, and I could finally get to sleep.

I did all that for a feeling that life was livable – a feeling that lasted no longer than five minutes. I often questioned whether those three hundred seconds of contented time were worth it.

Bingeing must be one of the loneliest things on the planet. I binged because I was lonely, and I never felt lonelier than when I binged. The food I was eating pushed me further and further into isolation. Although at times the urges were uncontrollable and the appetite insatiable, there were also times when it was so intense that I can remember each mouthful. I knew that eating was a decision I didn't want to make. I knew that I didn't want to put anything in my mouth. I knew that putting it in and chewing and swallowing was the complete antithesis of what I was trying to achieve. I knew that eating would make me fat and tip the delicate balance I managed to hold throughout each day. I knew that eating would inevitably lead to me hating myself and my body even more than before. And yet I kept putting things in my mouth.

The fact that no one could see it made it even worse. I never told anyone about the way I was punishing myself, for fear they might feel sorry for me. I had figured out by now that what I was now doing was called bulimia. All the magazine articles said to tell people about your struggles, but I couldn't do that because I wasn't worth it. I could never bring myself to tell the people I knew and trusted because my bingeing was indulgent, and I couldn't let anyone think that I was indulging in things I didn't deserve. I wanted people to think I was better and did a good job of convincing them. I couldn't even face telling Anne and Jayne about what I was doing in case they wouldn't want to know me anymore. I couldn't tell anyone that I'd failed and was doing something even more shameful. And I knew it didn't even make sense. How could I tell people that I, who had been so consumed with not eating, had suddenly started eating too much, and was scared by it? I hated deceiving them as much as I hated doing it, but it was a security blanket and I couldn't function without it.

As the months went by, I became more and more closed off inside my own food-filled world where calorie books and scales and curved mirrors all told me constant lies. In some ways, bulimia achieved what I had hoped. Obsessed with food and weight and fat and greed, I all but forgot what emotions were – apart from the intense self-hate that permeated my every waking minute.

I was in a swirling pit of despair and desolation and started to use things other than food and self-harm to express my hatred towards myself. I only allowed myself cold showers and refused to indulge in a haircut at a salon. The only distractions I allowed myself were books, which gave me short trips away into other worlds. I didn't even try to climb out of this despair – I couldn't see the possibility of life being any better. I wrote at the time:

> It's so strange, and very hard to describe. Anne and Jayne keep asking me if I want to get better, and whatever I answer, the truth is that I don't, not really. I would like to

be in a position to feel that I didn't have to deprive myself of food, but the truth is that, whatever people say, whatever help or treatment I have, I'm still going to be the same person, as horrible and undeserving as ever. Nothing's going to change that. Whatever happens, I still won't deserve any of the comforts of eating and a "normal" life. In a way, I really don't want any help, in case it lulls me into a false sense of security where I think I might be worth something, or in case someone actually convinces me of what I know to be wrong. I need to suffer – why can no one understand that? I need for people to see that I'm getting what I deserve, to comfort them, just so they know that I am aware of the horrible person that I am.

No one understands. No one understands that I just can't eat like everyone else does – they just don't get it. Neither do I, I just panic at the idea of it. Food keeps you going, and I don't want to keep going, I don't deserve to. I'm so huge – I want to be small again, back in the state where I was happy – I didn't hate myself then because I never considered it. I just had fun and did what I wanted to do. Now I can't, I'm too worried about what other people think of me – I can't let them see me rewarding myself. I need them to see what I truly deserve.

It sounds a bit like I was suicidal, but I wasn't. I didn't have the energy to be suicidal. In some ways suicide was the easy way out, and I hated myself too much to allow myself to take it. And, as always, I didn't want to let my parents down. I couldn't bear the idea of them blaming themselves for anything. Despite everything, I still wanted to be a model daughter. I knew that I wasn't, but at least I could pretend.

❀   ❀   ❀   ❀

"Abbie, I've got someone I want you to meet."

I was helping out at our church youth group and Mandy, the youth worker, called me in from supervising kids outside. Glaring, I jogged over to her – she knew I didn't like meeting new people.

"Abbie, this is Carys. I want you to go inside and get to know her. See you later!" Mandy shooed us towards her office, where I was left with a petite girl about my age, who seemed almost as uncomfortable as I was.

"Hi," she said, taking the initiative to cover my blank stare. "Sorry about that. Mandy can be quite forceful when she wants something!"

"I know that," I said, smiling slightly. "I've known her for a while. What I don't know is what she wants."

"She wants you to get better," Carys said.

I stared at her, speechless.

"Sorry, I know that was a bit blunt, but I didn't know what else to say. Mandy wanted me to talk to you because I've had anorexia, and she thought that I might be able to help. I'm not sure what she expects me to do, but you don't say no to Mandy!"

We laughed awkwardly at the truth behind what she'd said, and I perceived Carys' sincerity.

"No you don't," I agreed. "But I'm not anorexic, so I don't know what she expected you to do." I was trying to raise my defenses a bit, but I'd been so surprised by Carys' honesty that I was having trouble.

"You do have an eating disorder though, don't you?" she asked.

I was silent. I didn't want to admit it, but I found that I couldn't lie.

Carys filled the silence. "How about I share some of what I've been through, and then you can decide if you want to talk more?"

"Okay," I whispered, sitting down on one of the bean-bags Mandy kept in her office.

Carys spent the next hour or so telling me her life story, and how she'd struggled with an eating disorder for about ten years before making the decision to move towards recovering. I listened without interrupting until she talked about getting help.

"But how do you get help?" I asked. "I was in hospital, and it did more harm than good. I don't know how anyone gets better from anything in hospital."

"I was in contact with a charity called Kainos Trust. They help people like us to get better by running residential courses, where you can talk about things and learn about why we cope in the way we do and how to change that. They're in Gloucestershire, and they're running another course in a few weeks. I'll be going – do you want to come too?"

I felt bombarded. "I don't know. It's all a bit sudden. I'll think about it, okay?"

We chatted for a few more minutes before Carys looked at her watch.

"I have to go, sorry. Will you give me a ring sometime? I'd love to hear from you, really." She gave me a hug and her phone number and I walked her out to her car.

"I'll see you soon, okay?" she said before driving off.

I stood on the church steps watching her go and mulling over what she'd said. Mandy came over and put an arm around my shoulder.

"Do you forgive me?" she asked. "I know you don't like talking to people you don't know, but I thought it might help. Will you give the course at Kainos a try?"

Carys' car had disappeared around the corner, but I still stared after her. "I don't know. Let me think about it, okay?"

"Okay. But I am going to pester you about it. And I'm going to tell Anne and Jayne to pester you, too. I don't want to see you back in hospital. You need to get some help, Abbie, and soon."

Back at home, in the safety of my room, I thought it over some more. I wasn't convinced. It seemed like a lot of money for something that I knew wasn't going to help. I could see how it was possible for people like Carys to get better from eating disorders, but I couldn't see how it was possible for me to become a worthwhile person, which was really at the crux of it all. I hated what I was doing, but I did it because I hated myself – it was a vicious circle. I wrote about it in my journal to try and make sense of it:

> All these people who want me to go on this self-help week at Kainos need confronting. I need to ask them why they think I should go and what they think I'll get out of it. If they say they want to see me better I'll ask them why. If they ask me if I want to be better, I'll tell them "no." I'll ask them what they think "better" is, and whatever they say, I will tell them that it won't make me into a person who is worth anything – that they can't change. They want to try and raise my opinion of myself – well that won't work because whatever I think of myself, I'll still be horrible and undeserving, and I'd rather recognize that than cover it up and pretend.

Unable to stir up enough enthusiasm or hope in me to write to Kainos, Mandy, Jayne and Anne ended up writing the letter for me. I was so completely out of hope at that point that I just couldn't be bothered. I was also certain that these people at Kainos would declare me beyond help or a waste of their time, and I didn't think I could cope with that kind of rejection. It was one thing to think it for myself, but an entirely different kettle of fish to have other people say it. In the end, I went because the people who'd been looking out for me wanted me to, and I didn't want to let them down by telling them there was no hope. People gave money to Kainos on my behalf, which meant that finance wasn't a problem, and everyone was so encouraging that I felt I couldn't stay at home. So I got a week off work, packed my bags and told my parents that I was going to visit Ryan in Durham.

10

I set off for Gloucestershire in the small hours of the morning in my battered old car. I was full of apprehension. The journey was a nightmare, and I was stuck in traffic for over two hours. As I stared at the car in front of me, I thought back over the conversation I'd had with Anne the night before.

"I feel like such a fraud. I can't shake the feeling that there are people who are actually ill who really need the help. I feel like I'd be an impostor. I'm not ill, I'm just weak and have no willpower. Other people deserve their help far more than I do."

"But Abbie, you've tried on your own. This thing has a real hold on you. Kainos isn't just a godsend for other people, it can be a godsend for you too. You need to realize that you're ill, and you need some help to get better. Please, give it a go. If not for you, do it for me."

That was the push I needed – Anne had been so wonderful that I would have done anything for her. So, as my car chugged down the road towards Gloucestershire, I decided that I would give it my best shot. Anne was so often right that I made the decision to trust that she was right this time. I decided that I wouldn't waste the opportunity, or the money or time that people had donated to help this week away to happen. Somewhere in the back of my mind was a sprinkling of hope that things could be better than they were, and I knew that, if things were ever going to get better, Kainos was probably the place it was going to happen. I wanted God to work in my life, and I knew that I would need his help to make changes. So I steeled myself, gripped the steering wheel and drove determinedly into the uncertain.

When I finally reached Lower George House, a three-storey former pub and hotel that served as the headquarters of Kainos, I was met at the door by Nikki, who took me through to the kitchen to meet the other girls. My delays in traffic meant that I was last to arrive, and as I walked into the kitchen the chatter died down and the others turned to look at me. Nikki put a comforting hand on my shoulder.

"Abbie, these are the girls – Rachel and Lucy and Sally, and you know Carys." One by one, they all waved self-consciously.

"And this is Helena, our director."

Helena, a tall woman with curly hair, smiled warmly. "Hello Abbie, it's so nice to meet you. Would you like tea? Coffee?" She walked over and led me to an empty seat at the table.

"Water please," I whispered, not sure what I was supposed to do with myself or how to act. I sat next to a very pretty, dark-haired girl, who was about my age.

"I'm Lucy. Don't worry – I'm freaked out by it all too," she whispered.

I smiled gratefully and wrapped my hands around my glass. I listened in on the stilted conversations until Helena called us all to order and ushered us upstairs to the teaching room.

We sat in a semicircle at the front of the conference room, shuffling uncomfortably with our notebooks and pens, waiting for something to happen. Helena stood up and smiled.

"I want to welcome you all and tell you a bit about myself, and about what we do at Kainos. I was anorexic for a long time as a teenager, but started recovering when I became a Christian in hospital. I was always told that I would have to learn to live with anorexia, but I'm completely free. I knew when I recovered that I wanted everyone to know that there is such a thing as real and lasting freedom from eating disorders. If you take nothing else away from these few days, I pray that you'll always remember that – that you can be free." She paused for a moment. "I also want you to know that I understand that this is scary, and that many of you will feel that you aren't worthy or don't deserve to get help. I want to really encourage you to try and push those thoughts aside, just for the next few days, so you can take on board all the things that are said. If you're struggling with this, come and find one of us, and we'll do our best to talk it through with you."

Thoughts raced through my head. What Helena had just said rang clear and true. On the one hand, I wanted to get better and to take advantage of what was being offered. But the voices dripped constantly in my head like a Chinese water torture, telling me that I wasn't good enough, that I was a fraud and an impostor who didn't deserve to be well. But knowing that Helena had completely recovered from her anorexia meant that I knew I could trust her – everything she said came from a place of understanding – unlike the doctors who had asked me what I did and then told me why I did it. Kainos, Helena was telling us, had been set up in response to a call from God following her healing, and it was run specifically to help people like us. At Kainos I wasn't the odd one out – everyone was struggling, just like me. I decided that I would try really hard here to be open and honest.

Helena talked that first morning about food, and the concept that there is no such thing as "bad" food. Food is not something to be scared of, and not something that reflects my inner being. Rather, it is a fuel to keep me going – not something I deserve or don't deserve, but something my body, as a creation of God, requires.

Helena introduced us to methods for changing our eating habits gradually, which was a great help. I had decided long ago that my choices were either to eat and feel bad, or not eat and feel okay for a while. Helena introduced shades of grey to my black and white thinking about food. She acknowledged the power of food in our lives and that it wasn't easy. She also introduced the catchphrase of the week – "it's a process!" We laughed about it, but this was a very important idea to me. I saw what I did as silly. Other people managed fine – what was wrong with me that I couldn't conquer something that, for everyone else, was so easy? Helena and the other girls understood this struggle, helped me to stop berating myself for my inability to escape, and reassured me that my struggles were not trivial.

As Helena talked openly about her own battles I suddenly realized that I had relaxed and taken in more information than I'd expected to. Then, as she drew the session to a close, she said, "This is probably all the talking we're going to do about food. Tomorrow and in the days that follow we're going to look at the issues that keep you from being free from your eating disorders. It will probably be quite difficult, but it will be worth it."

My stomach dropped to my feet as we filed out to our cars, on to the next stop of the day.

❀   ❀   ❀   ❀

As I followed Nikki's car up to the end of a deeply rutted dirt lane, I wondered if my little old car and I were going to make it to the end of the week. As I rounded the last corner with apprehension, a beautiful cream house appeared, with a short, hazel-haired, motherly figure standing on the doorstep. As we all climbed out of our cars, avoiding the puddles and sheep droppings, she walked towards us with her arms outstretched.

"Welcome! I'm May! Let me show you around!" As soon as we'd taken our bags to our rooms and changed into more suitable shoes, we were given the grand tour.

"This is the kitchen. If you've never used an Aga before, this week will be your chance to learn," she smiled. "We'll all eat together in here – even if you don't eat. Meal times are about fellowship here, not food. And you can all be involved in cooking – it's a way of serving each other, and earning your keep!"

As we traipsed through the house and around outside, we couldn't help but start to catch May's enthusiasm.

"This is the vegetable garden," she said, gesturing proudly. "You've come in just the right season – we'll be picking all our vegetables for dinner!"

I looked out over the garden and caught sight of the River Severn just a few hundred yards away through the trees. "I could stay here forever," I thought.

As we made our way down to Lower George House the next morning for the second session with Helena, however, I became more and more apprehensive. What did she mean when she said that we would be covering issues other than food? Although I found the concept of eating quite frightening, I found her teaching on food and nutrition relatively easy to handle, because food was something I was used to thinking about. I knew food inside out. After all, I used it constantly to ward off other, more sinister, things – like feelings. All feelings, both good and bad, scared me. I didn't know how to deal with them. I didn't think I deserved to have good feelings, or to share my bad feelings, so the whole area of emotions was pretty much a non-starter for me. I was petrified that Helena was going to make me talk about my feelings, and I walked into the conference room as rigid with fear as I had been the previous day.

Surprise mingled with relief when Helena stood up and said, "Today we're going to talk about how we think. Pick up your Bibles and look up Romans twelve, verse two."

I flicked to the right page and found the phrase "be transformed by the renewing of your mind." As Helena spoke about how our thinking affects the way we function and how we deal with difficult things in our lives, I began to see that it was my beliefs about myself and about God that continued to fuel my struggles with eating and self-harm.

At first I didn't grasp the importance of this – I couldn't see the difference between feeling I was bad and thinking I was bad. But, over the next couple of days, I began to understand what Helena was talking about. Lucy and I had become fast friends, and we discussed this concept on a walk one afternoon.

"The thing about thinking is that it's logical," I said. "What we think is based on what we learn, on facts that can be either right or wrong. What we feel is different – it's based on how we respond to what we know or think we know. The problem is that if what we think and believe is wrong, our feelings will be all over the place. So to get better we need to make sure that what we believe is right, and then we know that our feelings will be more trustworthy. They might still be difficult to deal with, but at least they'll be right."

Lucy looked puzzled by my flash of inspiration. "But how do we know what's right to believe in and what isn't? I think I'd have problems with judging what's a good belief structure and what isn't."

I thought for a moment. "I guess you believe in sources that you know are more accurate than what's in your head. So we should be building our belief structure on what people we trust say to us, rather than taking for granted what's in our minds already."

Lucy paused, and then she brought up the valuable point we'd both somehow missed – despite the fact that Helena had spent all morning teaching it. "So trusting people like Helena and May is valuable, but the most valuable thing will be trusting what the Bible says – God's not going to be wrong!"

We wandered back along the river bank in amiable silence as I tried to make sense of what we had talked about.

"Abbie?" Lucy broke into my thoughts. "If you ever see that I'm acting on wrong beliefs, will you tell me? I don't think it's easy to see when it's yourself."

She bit her lip, as if she was nervous about asking me to do something for her and be involved in her life when the course was over.

"Of course," I said. "If you'll do the same for me."

We linked arms as if to seal the agreement, and a kindred friendship was born.

We arrived back in time to help with dinner. May encouraged us all to be involved in preparing meals. She taught us about ingredients, and how not to panic in the face of choices surrounding eating. We picked peas and beans and herbs and learned what to do with them, and we spent a lot of time in the kitchen around the enormous wooden table, enjoying the wood-burning smell of the Aga and the free flow of conversation. We talked about everything around that table – not just food, but everything that affected us, everything we wanted to achieve in life, and what we wanted to be when we grew up. We answered questions we didn't even know we had, and we learned to be honest with ourselves about how much of our lives we were unable to live because of our eating disorders.

Each day followed the same format, which was a comfort to the control freaks among us. We all got up for breakfast and sat around the table together, regardless of whether or not we ate anything. Then we set off for Lower George House and Helena's teaching, followed by lunch together. Afternoon activities varied, but they were purely intended for fun, which many of us had been depriving ourselves of for a long time. The staff did everything they could to encourage us to enjoy ourselves. After the evening meal, we gathered in the sitting room for a devotional time, sharing things that we'd learned, singing, and praying for one another. It was a beautiful end to each day, and I slept more soundly than I had in a long time.

As the week went on, I started to open up a little with members of the Kainos staff and with the other girls. Whether there was something about the beauty and welcoming nature of the Lower George and May's house, or whether it was just being with people who made the effort to tell me that they knew how I felt, I felt safe enough here to let down my defenses a bit. I began to talk about how I felt and admitted that my eating disorder and self-harm were beyond my control.

One afternoon, sitting outside chatting to May, I tried to describe to her one of the things I really struggled with – crying.

"It's not that I can't do it," I explained. "It's just that it seems like such an indulgence. I hate feeling like I'm a burden to people – I don't think I deserve it. And the truth is, if I started crying I'm not sure I could stop."

"So what do you do if you feel like you want to cry?" May asked.

"I cut myself. It's controlled, and it's predictable, and I don't have to take up anyone else's time when I do it."

May touched my arm. "But isn't it easier to let it out by crying than by hurting yourself? I don't think it's something I could do. Are you really that scared of crying?"

"It petrifies me. I might lose control. I'd rather shed blood than tears – it hurts less."

"How?"

I looked away. I didn't know.

11

I curled up tighter, pulling my knees up to my chin as I listened to the girls' voices ringing through the sitting room. I tried to join in, but I couldn't sing these words about coming to Jesus just as we are and mean them. I didn't feel I was acceptable to God – I couldn't grasp the idea that Jesus might love me just as I was. Why on earth would he want me? I wanted so much to give all of my life to him, and yet it felt impossible. I couldn't let anyone see all the muck and dirt that lay beneath the surface, especially not someone as perfect as Jesus.

The backs of my eyes began to prickle with tears, and I screwed my eyes shut and bit my lip to keep them from leaking out.

"Jesus really wants us, just as we are," May's voice broke into my thoughts. "It's only through giving our whole lives to him, and letting him in on the things we don't want him to see, that his love can shine through us. This song says it all – that Jesus will take us, just as we are, and turn us into beautiful gems. Shall we sing it again?"

As the other girls started singing again, I sat down. I dug my nails into my palms and concentrated on the pain. I let my ponytail down so that I could hide behind my hair, and I leaned forward so that no one could see my face.

"Abbie?" I felt a hand on my knee and opened my eyes to see May crouched on the floor in front of me. "Are you still with us?"

I moved my head, not sure whether the answer was yes or no, but letting her know that I was listening. The stinging in my palms was comforting, and the small amount of pain kept me grounded just enough to keep the tears away.

"Can I pray for you?" she asked gently.

I couldn't bring myself to look at her, but I nodded. She took my hand, and I felt Lucy move closer and put her hand on my back.

"Lord Jesus, I pray now that you would step into Abbie's life, and reveal yourself to her so that she can understand your love for her. I thank you that you loved her enough to die for her, and I pray that tonight she will begin to understand the worth she has as your daughter. I pray that you would release her from the feelings she's having now, and help her to express them safely. Thank you, Jesus, that you always hear our prayers. Amen."

As May finished praying, Lucy picked up her Bible. She read a passage I'd heard many times, but I'd never grasped the truth of it until that moment, when she replaced one word with my name. "For God so loved Abbie, that he gave his one and only son, that whoever believes in him shall not perish but have eternal life."

Lucy knelt down next to me and moved my hair away from my face. "That's you, Abbie. That's how much he loves you."

It was as if my insides were being ripped out. I simply could not comprehend how God could love me when I hated myself so much. I needed to cut, but I couldn't move – I knew that if I left everyone would know what I was doing. I was rigid with so many emotions – I couldn't even pick one out and name it. I was so tense I hurt all over. I clenched my teeth and squeezed my eyes shut, trying to keep the tears in and the world out.

"It's okay, Abbie," May said softly. "It's okay to cry and let it out."

I opened my eyes a sliver and saw May's kind brown eyes looking back. I couldn't help myself. As I felt the sob rising I gave in, though I felt like it was the end of the world.

I squeezed out a few words. "Please don't look at me. I just need to be in my own space. Please, don't notice me. I want to do this myself."

When May saw that I was serious she turned away and went back to the other girls.

With one hand still on my shoulder she spoke to the group. "What shall we sing next?"

After the session May slipped me a note, which I took up to my bedroom to read. I tried to imagine her reading it to me as I sat looking out over the dusky garden.

> Abbie – Deuteronomy 30:19 says this: "This day I call heaven and earth as witnesses against you that I have set before you life and death, blessings and cursings. Now, choose life, so that you and your children may live and that you may love the Lord your God, listen to his voice, and hold fast to him." God loves you, and wants the best for you, which will include giving up your eating disorder and self-harm at some point. But he's not going to take them away – the choice he is laying before you is between life and blessings in him, or death and cursings without. Choosing life is about choosing God, not about giving up everything else. Choose God, Abbie, and the rest will fall into place.

I felt the tears rising again, but this time they didn't seem so scary. I fell on my knees and started to weep. I knew that I wanted to choose God in a way that I had never done before. I had said before that I'd given my life to him, but I knew that it wasn't completely true because I'd refused to even talk to him about the things in my life I wanted to hide. At that moment, on the floor of the bedroom, I put my head in my hands and wept out my commitment to God.

"Jesus, my life is yours. I want to listen to your voice, and serve you. I want to be yours forever. Please forgive me for not choosing you before, and please help me to give my whole life to you. I want to be healthy for you but I don't know how. Please help me fight what's in my head. I love you Jesus. Amen."

The joy I felt as God touched me was almost tangible. I felt his arms gather me up like a child, and I felt his voice in my head, telling me that everything was all right, and that he loved me. For the first time I understood what it meant to be in God's presence, although I had heard the phrase at church many times. All the emotions I had been holding in for so long started to come out as I laughed and cried at the same time. I could have stayed on the floor like that forever, but eventually I picked myself up, brushed my hair and washed the tearstains off my face.

As I walked downstairs for evening drinks I felt different – somehow lighter. Knowing that I had someone on my side in the fight made me feel stronger. Whenever I thought again about how much Jesus loved me and what he'd done for me – both on the cross and in my room – my eyes welled up and tears streamed down my face.

I walked into the kitchen and saw Lucy sitting at the table reading. "You okay, Abbie? Anything I can do?"

"I'm fine. I know it doesn't look like I am, but I really am! I'm happy, and comfortable – I don't know why I keep crying."

May came up behind me and put a hand on my shoulder. "Sometimes an experience with God does that. It's so awesome that sometimes it takes a while for all the emotions to work their way out. You've got a lot of years of tears stored up in those eyes of yours!"

We started making tea and the others drifted in to talk about their days. An evening "de-brief" had become tradition among us, and praying just before bed encouraged a good night's sleep. Everyone shared a little about their day – what they had learned, what they'd enjoyed, and some of the things they'd struggled with. We really connected as a group, and by this point in the week we were sharing all sorts of things that we'd never have dreamed of talking about in the "real" world.

My tears brought lots of comic relief that evening, because every time someone said or did something positive, I began to cry again as I remembered the amazing things that Jesus had done for me. The girls teased me laughingly.

"You don't need to put the hot water on for baths tonight, May," said Carol. "Abbie can fill them all!"

Although I felt a bit embarrassed about my sudden outbursts, I was able to laugh along with the others. I went up to bed feeling freer than I had in years, and I slept through the entire night for the first time in months.

That evening was a turning point. That one prayer turned on a switch in my head that enabled me to look forward to going home and starting a new and normal life. I wanted to leave Gloucestershire a different person and go home to a different way of life. I still found the idea of going home very scary, but it was scary with anticipation. I'd learned so much from Helena – about how to change my belief structure, how to deal with negative emotions in a healthy way, and what it means to be spiritually healthy. It actually did seem possible that I could recover and life could be better. The encounter I'd had with God that last evening invigorated me to put all my newfound knowledge into practice. I was probably too enthusiastic – I was so excited to start a life without starving and cutting that I didn't really think about the reality of what might happen when I hit the first bumps in everyday life.

But at the same time I was also frightened. I had no idea how I was going to cope on my own, without the support and secure environment that Kainos offered. I found it difficult to picture what life would be like without food and self-harm occupying my mind, and I couldn't conceive of being at home without my eating disorder to fall back on. I wanted to make the changes, but I didn't know how to go about it.

I wasn't the only one experiencing these mixed emotions, and on the last day we looked at how to manage a life of recovery in place of a life ruled by an eating disorder. Helena and I sat cross-legged on the floor on Friday morning, writing out a plan for how to cope at home.

"It's about planning how you're going to deal with the difficult things that come up in normal, everyday life, Abbie. From what you've said it seems like you find it hard to set boundaries – around food, around people, around everything. You also need to think about how you'll deal with negative emotions, and figure out a list of alternatives to starving, bingeing and cutting. If you can write yourself a plan for how to manage your life when you get home, you'll have something to fall back on."

I could see the wisdom in Helena's instruction, and by the end of the two-hour session I had a "going-home plan". I set myself boundaries around how much was enough work to do, how much I allowed other people to hurt or upset me, and how to say no to other people when I didn't feel I could do what they asked. I also had an eating plan, so that I didn't have to make so many decisions about food – something that had been my downfall before. I planned a structure for my days, including things that would make recovery an easier ride. I also set myself weekly goals – small steps that would lead me closer and closer to being better without being so scary that they were unreachable. The plan incorporated physical, emotional and spiritual steps, and we designed it so that I could revisit and change it.

Having all of this set out in a logical, step-by-step guide helped me to believe that I could apply everything I'd learned to my everyday life. When I carried it out of the front door on my way home, it didn't seem like an impossible feat. I drove home believing that I could do it, that life would only go on and up from there. I wrote to Helena as soon as I got home. I wanted her to know how much I appreciated everything I'd been taught and I wanted to confide in her some of the less obvious changes in me. I included the following:

> This time last week, I wouldn't have been able to run upstairs,
> In case someone heard me and recognized I was there.
> This time last week, I wouldn't have been able to sit in the sun,
> Because I enjoy it, and I didn't deserve enjoyment.
> This time last week, I wouldn't have been able to sit with people,
> In case they looked at me and hated me.
> This time last week, I wouldn't have been able to talk to anyone,
> In case they saw me for what I really was.
> This time last week, I wouldn't have been able to serve myself food,

In case I took more than others thought I deserved.
This time last week, I wouldn't have been able to pray aloud for others,
In case I said the wrong thing.
This time last week, I wouldn't have been able to copy a recipe,
Because I didn't deserve the joy of cooking it.
This time last week, I couldn't have said thank you for food,
Because I hated the power it had over me.
Now, there's been a change.
I can run upstairs purely because I have something to do.
I can sit in the sun, because God made it for me to enjoy.
I can enjoy a conversation, and not be scared of saying something.
I can think I might be of use to someone else, or me.
I can take food, because God created my body to need its fuel.
I can pray for others, because God wants to provide for our needs.
I deserve to cook for myself and others.
I deserve to speak and be heard.
I deserve to listen to myself.
I deserve to be contented.
I deserve to eat, and
I want to say thank you.

12

As soon as I had unpacked, I headed into the kitchen to tell my mum the truth about what I'd been doing for the past week.

"I wasn't really visiting Ryan in Durham," I said. "I was in Gloucestershire doing a residential course for people with eating disorders. I'm sorry I didn't tell you."

Once she got over the shock, Mum was very supportive of what I'd done. She still didn't know the full extent of what had been going on for the past few years but, after reading the going-home plan I'd produced, she went out of her way to make things easy for me. She took me shopping and she encouraged me to spend time with her and my friends rather than alone in my room.

"I'm proud of you," was one of the few things she said – and one of the most important.

In spite of her support, maintaining the changes and living the lessons I'd learned proved much harder than I'd expected. Kainos had provided a very structured environment and a strong network of people who were constantly there to talk to about things. Although I came back to a fantastic support network, I also came back to the life that had fed my eating disorder in the first place. It was much easier being well in the safe world of Lower George House, where there were no outside pressures.

There were some great things about coming home, and some goals that I found easier than others. I started to do things for pleasure, like going to the cinema and having my hair cut by a hairdresser – and I enjoyed them without berating myself. I reminded myself that God made me as lovingly as he made every other individual, and I put a saying on my wall that reminded me that God invented small pleasures and rejoices when we delight in them.

However, as I wrote to Helena:

> I can't say that it's all a bed of roses – for example, food is still a big issue. The physical issues, and trying to learn about what my body needs, are proving really challenging – because I've lost recognition of how my body works. I'm still finding out how much I need to eat when, what having an appetite feels like, and what foods I do and don't like – although it's now much easier to eat the ones I do like, rather than finding things I don't like to eat as punishment. I'm finding mealtimes really hard – I still can't be social over food, and want mealtimes to be over as quickly as possible. Each meal is a struggle – I pray with every swallow and need at least an hour's distraction after each one. But I'm experimenting and trying and learning that one failure isn't the end of the world.

> And I know God's on my side, and he keeps letting me know he's there! He really does work in people's lives – I always knew that. But I didn't ever believe until a few weeks ago that he would work in my life. It just didn't occur to me. But it's true – he will work for good in all those who have faith in him. I'm learning, albeit slowly, that God and I have a really good thing going here. I trust and he does – we're a really good team.

I managed to sustain some of the changes I'd made. I ate better than ever before, although it wasn't always easy –

and I rarely binged. Cutting myself took a backseat to other, much healthier, coping mechanisms, like walking, singing and reading. The problems with food didn't go away immediately, and it was hard work to keep making healthy choices. God gave me different supports to help – the love of my mum and my friends, who listened when I was struggling, and all the lessons I'd learned at Kainos. I also had willpower – I realized that the longer I could abstain from bingeing and cutting, the easier it became not to revert to these behaviors. I knew that every time I succumbed to the temptation, resisting would become harder again, and I didn't want that. Despite my best efforts, I hadn't been able to completely leave these things behind, and I still gave in every so often, but I now had tools to deal with those times.

❀   ❀   ❀   ❀

One of the things that made it difficult to stay on an even keel was living with my dad. His drinking had got steadily worse, and I found it very hard to cope with him being drunk. I tried to talk to my mum about it, but I just couldn't understand it.

"Why?" I cried. "Why does he feel he has to drink? Doesn't he realize how difficult it makes it for everybody?"

"I don't think he thinks he can help it. It's like a quick-fix solution for him – drinking makes the world go away for him for a while," Mum explained patiently.

"But he's always saying how sorry he is and how much he loves us, and he promises not to do it again, and then it seems to make no difference. Why can't he realize how much it hurts everyone and get some help?"

"I don't know, darling. Just be patient and stay out of his way if you can. I don't want anything to be hard for you right now. You're doing so well." Mum held me close, and I leaned on her shoulder.

"I don't understand why he doesn't just stop if he hates hurting us as much as he says he does." My words were muffled by her soft sweater.

Mum just hugged me.

At the time I couldn't see just how similar I was to my dad, and I never realized how much my own self-destructive behavior was hurting my mum.

I also talked to my friend Matt, with whom I sang in a local choir, about my dad.

"It just bugs me. I don't know how to stay out of his way, and I hate never being able to have people around."

Matt's answer seemed simple and scary all at the same time. "My roommate's just moved out – why don't you take the second bedroom?"

It was all agreed upon that night, and within a few weeks I'd signed a contract and moved in.

Despite the fact that I was one hundred percent enthusiastic about moving out, friends like Anne and Jayne were unsure if it was a wise move. Jayne, always logical and never afraid to tell me the truth, was particularly concerned about how I would cope.

"I know you've made lots of changes since Kainos, Abs, but you're not there yet. Are you sure you can keep up the changes living on your own?"

I could see where she was coming from, and I was torn. "I know I'm not completely better, but I can't keep living in that house. I spend all day wondering what state my dad's going to be in when he walks through the door. I can't live like that – the stress makes it so much harder to stay healthy."

"I can see that it's hard, but don't you think it will be harder to be in a place where you don't have a routine to fit into, where you're your own boss? You're going to have to work really hard to keep structured enough to stay on top of everything."

I saw the concern in Jayne's eyes, and I knew she was right. I was still tempted not to eat on many occasions, and I still needed frequent pep talks about my worth and importance. And although I wasn't self-harming as much as I had been before, I still caused myself physical pain of some sort when I felt I couldn't cope. Although I hated eating meals with my family, the structure of home and my overriding concern not to worry my mum played a big part in my effort to stay healthy.

Still, it seemed that moving out was the lesser of two evils, since my dad's alcoholism made my emotional state as tentative as it had ever been. I was truly co-dependent – I never knew what my mood was going to be until I knew how dad was, and so I was constantly anxious. This wreaked havoc with many of the plans I had made at Kainos. Meals were sometimes thrown together or missed entirely because of dad's drinking episodes. I could never completely relax or feel calm in my own home, which meant that keeping my eating and self-harm under control was almost impossible.

Unsure whether to stay or go, I decided to give it a try and to keep in close touch with people about how I was feeling. With my going-home plan from Kainos firmly in my hand, I was positive, hopeful and determined to make it on my own as I moved into my new place.

Matt's place wasn't big, but it felt like home. It was my first grown-up home – I wasn't a student, and I wasn't in a crummy student house. In my enthusiasm I persuaded Matt that we should redecorate. We painted the kitchen a vibrant sunny yellow with bright blue detail, and we did the living room in rich African colors with a very big, very squishy, dark red sofa. I would spend hours curled up in its womb-like cushions, wishing that I could stay there forever, away from the world. We spent my first few weeks there painting, but it was worth it – when we finished it was a work of art with personality that drew me eagerly in from work each night.

My bedroom was the smaller of the two, and I loved it because it was my own. I worked hard to earn the money to pay for it, and it was my space. I took a break from unpacking to survey my new bedroom and drink in this new sense of independence. It all seemed too good to be true. I muttered a quick prayer, "Lord, please don't let me mess this up."

❀   ❀   ❀   ❀

Within a few weeks, I came to the realization that living on my own was harder than I thought it would be. Although I was relieved to be away from my family and the struggles with my dad, I missed the structure of family life. I'd worked hard to get over my eating disorder so I could experience the life other people my age were leading. I was free to do anything I wanted! But the same freedom that had seemed so attractive and exciting eventually became a major problem. There were too many choices. I didn't know how to live on my own. I didn't know enough about a normal everyday life to begin living one. The kinds of choices I faced would have been basic and inconsequential for most people, but for me they were complicated equations to which I could find no answers. Should I put the blue or the white covers on my bed? Which pot should I use for cooking the pasta? Should I read my book in the evening, or watch a movie, or go out? Every decision was riddled with anxiety. When Matt was around I could do what he did, but he worked much longer hours than I did and he was out most evenings. When I was alone, indecision plagued me.

During this time I learned to take some risks and try things I hadn't done before. Some of these were healthy, such as letting someone else order food for me – some, like smoking marijuana just for kicks, were less healthy. Freedom allowed me to make mistakes, but therein lay the problem. When most people make mistakes they learn what to do or not to do next time. When I made a mistake it was a failure, and even after my time at Kainos I still berated myself for my mistakes. I couldn't see that making mistakes is a normal part of every human life. Each decision loomed before me like a huge scary monster just waiting to eat me up and make a failure out of me. The most important thing I learned at Kainos – that I was never going to be perfect – was the first thing I forgot.

Not knowing how to deal with making decisions left me panicky, but instead of keeping the promise I'd made to talk to people about how I was feeling, I kept it all inside. Anne and Jayne both gave me plenty of opportunities to tell them how I was feeling, but I punctuated our conversations with phrases like "I'm fine," and "I'm doing really well." All the while, these emotions were secretly bubbling away just under the surface and I felt completely out of control. I chose not to deal with things rather than risk making a wrong decision.

These feelings inevitably led me back to what I knew. I was still following my going-home plan, but I started making little nips and tucks – a little less carbohydrate here, a missed snack there. I told myself it was nothing, but somewhere in the back of my mind I knew that I was at the edge of a slippery slope.

"It'll be fine. I won't go overboard. I'll just lose a little bit of weight, just cut down a bit until I feel calmer. It'll all be okay," I reassured myself.

So I cut out bread, then potatoes, and almost immediately I felt better. Controlling my eating calmed my anxiety, as I knew it would, and as a result I found every other decision much easier.

The problem this time was that I knew I was flailing. I just couldn't cope with all the variation of a normal life. I still sought complete control over everything that happened to me. In the impossibility of this, I was able to make my food intake bear the brunt of the discomfort. And so I slipped neatly back into disordered eating. I didn't lose much weight initially, and my eating probably looked pretty normal to most people, but I knew it was unhealthy – if not physically, then definitely emotionally.

The only thing I was certain of at this point was that I didn't want anyone to know I wasn't coping. I didn't want to let people down by falling back into anorexia. I knew that it was possible to stave off my eating disorder, because I'd done it before, in the hospital. Desperate to keep my eating patterns healthy, I made the conscious decision to switch to self-harm instead.

13

I sat on my bed and stared up at the ceiling, trying to gather thoughts as they flitted through my head. I suddenly noticed how blue the room was – the walls were blue, and my blue lampshade cast a bluish haze over the room. I could have been swimming in blue – everything seemed that vague – and blue. The room looked blue, smelled blue, tasted blue, felt blue. I had read somewhere that blue was calming. But here I was – calm and yet torn apart, safe and yet full of fear and neuroses. This blue room was a stronghold and a jail, my haven and my hell.

It was twenty to ten – about the time I always cut – and everything was set out just right. My lamp shone dimly, just enough to light up the blades, gauze, tape and scissors laid out in perfect parallel beside me on my bed. The blade was a new one, chosen carefully from a selection I kept in a special box by my bed. I never used the same blade twice. Unwrapping a new blade from its waxed-paper covering felt like getting a present. My childlike excitement rose as I moved closer to the moment I would finally feel okay again. It was like looking forward to my sixth birthday, knowing that we were going to the cinema for a special treat.

I stroked the skin on my tummy, finally finding a section that wasn't covered in small, parallel cuts. I took the blade between two fingers, and, pulling the skin taut with the other hand, drew the blade across the skin. I didn't wait to find out if once was enough. I drew again and again, producing a necklace of lines hung with red beads. As the blood began to flow down towards the sheets I covered the cuts with a tissue and leaned back. I closed my eyes and let the satisfying haze engulf me. The backs of my eyelids were blue too, just like the room.

Minutes or hours later, I cleaned away the blood with a bottle of mineral water and gauze and applied antiseptic cream and a dressing.

Finally, I could sleep.

❀   ❀   ❀   ❀

It seems bizarre now to think of my self-harm as a choice, because most of my memories are of feeling unable to do anything else. Cutting was a compulsion – if not medically speaking, then certainly in my mind. But I knew the consequences. I knew that once I started I'd struggle to stop, I knew that I would become secretive again, and I knew that it was wrong. On some level, I even knew that I had the choice of being honest with people and saying I couldn't cope, but I didn't entertain that option. Instead, I decided that I would avoid everything difficult and uncomfortable by cutting myself, thereby putting on an exterior of normality maintained by insanity.

That blue bedroom was where I built my self-harm home. Cutting was something I did entirely for myself, and over time it became ritualistic in its simplicity. Living essentially on my own allowed my descent back into self-harm – Matt being out most of the time meant that I had the space to foray into my own head. Cutting became an obsession – no other thoughts could ease their way into my mind. It was an affair with my own body that insidiously pervaded everything I did, said and thought. When I wasn't doing it I was thinking about it, fantasizing, imagining grandiose pictures of bleeding onto my bedroom floor.

The main attraction of cutting was its intimacy. I didn't care about sex – it was never a temptation for me the way it was for my peers. I lived out my longing, my passion, my every exhilaration and desolation, in my love affair with my own skin. The eroticism of cutting is haunting; it is beyond any other intimacy. It is a oneness with the inner workings of the human body, and perhaps even soul, as the very essence of life is spilt in the swiftest move of a razor. It is hypnotizing and haunting, setting the precedence for all relationships to come – none of which will ever reach the exquisiteness of seeing yourself laid bare. At the moment of the act itself, there is nothing more to know.

I was so completely absorbed with self-harm that everything else in my life seemed to float away and so, despite all my better judgements and hollow promises, anorexia needled its way back into my life. I was so consumed by the need to cut that I didn't have the time or spare emotion to eat. I started losing weight because I didn't eat – as opposed to not eating to lose weight. I was too immersed in the song I was singing with self-harm to think about eating – the way you don't eat when you're in the middle of your finals, or in love.

❀   ❀   ❀   ❀

One day, sitting at the dinner table at Anne's house, I was hit with sudden horror by the ham on the plate in front of me. Before I'd had time to process the thought, the words had come out.

"I can't eat that."

Anne looked puzzled. "Are you having a rough day, Abs? Do you want a smaller bit?"

I tried to make sense of it, but I couldn't. I could feel myself beginning to panic.

"No. I just can't eat it." I shook my head.

Anne took me over to the sofa and sat me down, holding my hands to keep them from shaking.

"Is it the whole meal? Is it too much? What can I do to make it easier?" Her eyes searched mine as she tried to make sense of my outburst.

"It's the ham." I shuddered as I said it, tasting the word in my mouth. "I can't eat it. I don't know why. It's just wrong, and I can't."

After half an hour of trying and failing to talk it out, we gave up and I had cheese instead. Neither of us realized what was beginning.

Over the next few weeks, as if controlled by some remote force, I became rigid about what I could eat when. I found foods that were "safe" and became obsessed with them. I began to eat the same things at the same time every day. For a while it was a whole wheat roll with low-fat cottage cheese, then I switched to a leek and potato soup that came in powdered form. I would always have the soup in the same cup and add lots of salt before the water. I went through a phase of eating one particular supermarket prepared salad, and then I switched to slices of tomato smothered with salt. I dined each night on a plateful of frozen chopped spinach and cauliflower florets, microwaved to within an inch of their lives. As my fears surrounding food grew, it suddenly mattered what order I put things on the plate and where on the plate they were. I couldn't eat one kind of food if it had touched another food on the plate, and I had to get the food in my mouth without it touching my lips.

This obsessive-compulsiveness around food was completely new. I knew it was crazy, and I knew that it made no sense, but everything about me felt wrong if I didn't eat the right things in the right way at the right time. I could feel the chaos in my head building, and the only things I could make predictable were my eating and cutting rituals. The knowledge that I was in control of something, even if I had no control of my emotions and the mess inside my head, gave me the ability to keep going. I became so disciplined, so inflexible, that I couldn't see how I was hurting myself and those around me.

❁　❁　❁　❁

"I've had an idea," Anne said when I turned up at her house one night after work.

"That sounds worrying. Did it hurt?" I was hoping the sarcasm might deflect what I imagined was going to be an idea I wouldn't really like.

Anne rolled her eyes. "Ha ha. I thought we could set up a meal rota so you don't have to cook or eat by yourself. What do you think?"

I was troubled. "I don't know. It sounds scary."

Anne looked at me steadily.

"I don't want to. Is that a good enough reason?" I asked.

Anne took my hands in hers. "Here's the situation as I see it. You're losing weight – really quite quickly. You may think I don't notice, but I do – it's pretty obvious. I'm not expecting you to see it, because your image of yourself is all skewed. So I'm asking you to trust me. The thing is, if you keep going the way you are, you'll end up back in the hospital, and there'll be nothing we can do about it. Do you agree with me so far?"

I looked away, but my silence said everything. In the remote corner of my mind that was still working rationally, I knew she was right.

"So," she continued, "I was thinking I'd ask five women from church if they would each feed you one night a week. It means you could eat with a family and copy what they eat, and you'd have someone with you afterwards for the high-risk time. They could pray with you, and stop you from being sick or self-harming. What do you think? I could organize it all for you. Do I have your blessing?"

I turned back to face her. "You have my permission. I'm reserving the blessing for now."

She smiled. "That's good enough for me."

By the following week, the plan was in place. All five women were amazing. They put up with having their family lives disrupted for a night while they comforted, held, encouraged and reassured me. Although eating felt impossible at times, I did it because I didn't want to let them down – and also because, in many ways, I was relieved to have it taken out of my hands. Some days were harder than others, but overall it meant that my weight and energy levels stayed high enough to work, and I was able to keep going that little bit longer.

But apart from these evening meals I intentionally kept myself isolated. I consented to the meal rota to please Anne – I would much rather have stayed away from people so that they didn't have to see me. I hated how I looked, and I hated all the attention. I wasn't worth being looked after in other people's houses. I stopped socializing in the evenings and drove around London alone instead, just to have something to do with my hands. I didn't even phone my mum or go to see her because I didn't want her to worry about me – she had her hands full with my dad. I didn't want to risk seeing my dad, either – I didn't have the energy for the shouting matches that usually ensued. I thought it would be easier if I just stayed out of the way.

Unfortunately, Anne's rescue plan came a bit too late. I had already fallen too far inside my own head to escape, and I continued to crumble. Despite, or perhaps because of, my improved eating habits, my cutting spiraled out of control. The love affair became all the more sordid as I gave up caring about scarring and about people seeing. I cut as much as I wanted for the sheer hell of it. I crashed through all of my own boundaries and lost the control I was so desperately trying to cling to.

I sat in bed one night looking at the virginity of my forearm, and I couldn't resist. I don't know what it was about my arm that made me want to cut it so desperately – maybe it was just that it looked so clean. I ventured into it slowly, with just one cut that I would work deeper and deeper, re-opening every time, to avoid the kind of scarring that I knew would alert people to my inability to cope. Before long, I had fabricated an excuse to keep my arm constantly bandaged so I could cut as much as I wanted without anyone knowing. My arm was crisscrossed with cuts of varying age and deepness, a constant reminder of the paradox – I was a mess, but I could cope. I fell into an abyss as my cutting became all-consuming, leading up to the episode with the hammer. Even though I didn't actually do any real harm that day besides the usual cuts, I knew that it signaled the end. I knew I wouldn't survive much longer, and I gave up.

Although I began cutting to clear my mind, the mess in my head and the mess of my behavior got worse together. The rituals I clung to, rather than easing the

emotional pain I was feeling, just added to the cacophony. Emptying myself of food so that I could feel
empty of emotion was not working anymore. This structure for coping that I had fabricated suddenly gave way
like the proverbial house built on the sand. Instead of
recognizing this and stopping the cutting, I decided that
I just wasn't doing it enough – and so it escalated
beyond all constraints I had previously put in place.
Negative emotions ruled me. I couldn't escape the
shouting in my head: "You'll never be good enough!
You're disgusting, selfish, and a burden on everyone
you know!"

Only when I punished myself by not eating could I
quiet the voice for a little while. When I was empty of
food I felt unpolluted. If I'd been able to have it my way
there would have been nothing at all. No body, nothing
material that could be soiled, just that part of me that
nothing could touch. I wanted to shrink until I was
unnoticeable and could just cease to be. My connection
to everyday life had all the strength and substance of a
thread. I cut every day and snuck out to the stockroom
at work if I couldn't wait until I got home. Sitting on a
stool behind the counter I dug into my skin with my
nails and, if I needed to, pressed into the previous
night's cuts as hard as I could to get myself back to the
real world.

Once home I could actively hate myself. I detested
what I'd become and the disgusting behaviors and
secrecy that ruled my life, but I couldn't resist. I felt that
if I didn't do these things everything would completely
fall apart. I couldn't be more specific than "everything,"
and I couldn't describe what falling apart would look
like. All I knew for sure was that my existence was hanging in the balance, and it was only by cutting and not
eating that I could keep the scale straight. I knew that if

anyone expressed warmth towards me it was only because I had deceived them by not allowing them to see what a foul, disgusting person I was. I was sure that if I told anyone what I was going through they would desert me – and I wouldn't have blamed them.

Everything about my self-harm was secretive, partly because I couldn't bear to admit to anyone what I was doing, but also because I wanted to keep it for myself. It was a love-hate relationship – I hated myself for loving something that I knew was intrinsically wrong and anti-humanity. I was captivated in the way I might have been by a lover – all I could think about was when I might see my blades again and fall into their arms, feeling nothing but the meshing of the two of us together. The love was so intense and the thought of giving it up so painful. I chose to keep cutting, and yet suffered, becoming a shell of a person, torn apart because I knew that the thing I wanted most was wrong. Issues of faith, survival and desire overwhelmed and paralyzed me. The only time anything felt real was when I was cutting.

When I couldn't face being on my own at home I went to Anne's house and curled up on her squishy yellow sofa. I spent hours and hours there, not talking to anyone. Her kids thought of me as an extra sister; I was the "honorary" member of the family. They accepted me whatever state I was in, and I could say things to Anne that I couldn't say to anyone else. She was never disgusted, never gave up or lost patience with me, and she was the only person who didn't have any expectations of me.

One day I phoned her from home in a state.

"I can't cope. I'm on my own and I'm scared to move. I've cut, and I can't stop cutting. I don't trust myself to do anything. I don't want to die, but I can't go on. Please help me." I couldn't decide whether I was crying, hysterical or calm. My voice echoed in the empty chamber of my head.

"Stay where you are. Don't move. I'll be there in ten minutes."

I buzzed her in and curled up in a corner. I wasn't sure whether I could be rescued. I doubted I was worth the effort.

"I'm sorry, I'm sorry, I'm sorry, I'm sorry," I repeated. I didn't trust myself to stay silent, and I had nothing else to say.

Anne picked me up off the floor, whispering soothingly into my hair.

She cleared up my cutting stuff, washed out my bloody clothes and dressed my arm. She didn't say anything to challenge me and she didn't ask me why, she just said not to worry – it would be okay. She sat on the sofa holding me for half an hour, until I calmed down enough to form sentences.

"I'm sorry. I didn't mean to put you through this. I'm such a nightmare. I hate myself for doing this to you. I'm so horrible – such a horrible waste of space."

The tears sliding down Anne's face shocked me. She struggled to speak. "I just wish you could see what I see. I hate what you're doing to yourself."

I was horrified – I hated myself for making her cry.

She gathered herself together and wiped her tears. "I know you can't stop yet, but I really wish you could. I wish you could understand that you are so beautiful and I love you so much. There's nothing I can do, I know that, but I wish I could."

❈   ❈   ❈   ❈

Eventually, I lost it. Like an ice cream cone in the sun, I started dripping and once I started I couldn't stop. I had a complete melt-down. One morning, while driving to work, I blacked out. I didn't crash the car – it was more of a daydreaming space-out. The last thing I remembered was stopping suddenly at a set of traffic lights to let a woman pushing a baby cross in front of me. I may have blinked, I don't know, but when I opened my eyes I didn't know where I was or what to do. So I kept driving. I couldn't make a decision to stop, or turn, so I just drove straight until I reached a crossroad. I sat there until someone honked behind me. I looked at the signs and realized that if I turned left I could get onto the London Orbital and keep driving round and round without having to make a decision.

So that's what I did – until nine o'clock that night. I spent thirteen hours driving around, stopping only to get coffee and fuel. I have no idea what I thought about, or if I thought at all. Eventually I realized: this is what people do when they are crazy.

14

I woke up in a strange room. As I came to I remembered arriving at Lucy's house the night before, where Lucy's mum Pam had given me an understanding hug and put me to bed. I rubbed the sleep from my eyes and realized I'd had my first dreamless sleep in weeks.

As the world came into focus I tried to make some sense of what was going on in my head. I was sort of surprised that I didn't feel as if the world had ended. Instead, I was overwhelmed by this feeling of nothingness. It was as if my mind, in an act of self-preservation, had removed all feelings about everything – except the omnipresent guilt and self-hatred.

I sat on the pink bedspread, trying to figure out what to do. I hadn't showed up at work the previous day, and I hadn't been in contact with anyone for over 24 hours. I knew Matt would be worried and Anne would be phoning around everyone on my meal rota list to see if they'd heard anything. I hadn't seen my parents in ten days, and I had no idea what was going on with them. I felt so guilty and stupid. I couldn't believe how inconsiderate I'd been – it was so unlike me to forget about the people I cared about. I was so busy dealing with my own head that I'd completely forgotten that anyone might be worried. That fact hit home more sharply than anything had for a long while. I was in a mess I couldn't get out of, and I needed help.

"Abbie? Are you awake? Are you okay? I need to go to work soon. What do you want to do today?"

The door creaked open an inch, and Pam stuck her head around the door to see me sitting at the top of the bed fully dressed, chin on knees, trying to decide what to do.

"How are you feeling this morning?"

I didn't want to make eye contact. "Stupid. Embarrassed. Empty. I don't really know."

"Do you think you can face work?" she asked.

"I don't want to see anyone," I shuddered. "But what else would I do?" The idea of going back to my real life at all seemed preposterous. I just wanted to stay where I was, comforted by the pink bedspread drawn up around my knees.

"Take a sick day. Phone someone, see someone, aim to not be alone?" Pam suggested.

I turned the idea around in my head. Was I sick enough to take a sick day? I suddenly noticed that I was pinching at my arms to keep my mind on the matter at hand, and I realized the answer was yes.

"I'll go to Anne's. She's not working today. I'll phone work and then go to Anne's."

Pam kissed the top of my head. "I'm sorry I have to go. Will you phone me later?"

I nodded, not sure what I would have to tell her.

❀   ❀   ❀   ❀

I stood dripping at Anne's front door, soaked by the spring rain. Even before she opened the door I could see the relief on her face through the glass. She didn't say a word as she ushered me through the door and guided me to the yellow sofa. She sat me down and knelt to take off my wet shoes.

"I don't know what to say." My voice didn't sound like me – it had a flat quality I'd never heard before.

Anne smoothed damp hair tendrils from my face. "Then don't say anything yet. Just sit. I'm going to make a couple of phone calls."

I don't know how long she was gone, or who she called. When she came back she brought a mug of tea.

"I think you need to warm up and get some sugar in you. Please drink it, and we can talk about what happens now."

I took the tea, grateful for something to warm my hands on if nothing else.

"What's been going on, Abs?"

I described the last couple of days to her – the number of times I'd cut, how little I'd eaten, how I'd blacked out, and how I'd driven around for hours before ending up at Lucy's. When I'd finished I sat back and waited. Surely Anne would think I was completely crazy and give up on me. She sat and thought for a moment before speaking.

"I think I want to phone someone and ask their advice. Is it okay if I call Helena at Kainos and ask what she thinks would be a good thing to do?" she asked.

I couldn't really see the point but I nodded as Anne reached for the phone and dialed the number. She started to speak, but I couldn't concentrate. Every time I tried to focus, the words she was saying blurred into a jumble of sound. I closed my eyes until I felt Anne's hand on my shoulder and saw her holding out the phone. I took it and put it to my ear.

"Abbie?" I heard the note of concern in Helena's voice.

"Hi," I whispered.

"I think it would be sensible for you to go to the hospital, just to see what they think. I'm worried, and

Anne's worried, and we think it would be good to get an opinion from a doctor. Is that okay with you?"

I shrugged.

"Abbie?"

I realized Helena wouldn't have heard my reaction.

"I shrugged. I really don't care about anything, so I guess that makes it a good idea."

"Okay. Phone me later and let me know how you get on. Okay?"

"Okay. Bye."

Anne sat beside me and put my cup of tea back in my hands. I took a sip. It tasted like molasses and stuck to my throat.

"Finish that, and then we'll go, alright? Are you holding up?"

I leaned on her shoulder, too emotionally exhausted to hold my head up. "Being in the world is just too hard."

❀   ❀   ❀   ❀

We'd been looking at the grey walls of the waiting room at the local mental health offices for nearly three hours, and we still hadn't seen anyone other than the receptionist who showed us in. Anne had gone on yet another search to find out if anything was happening anywhere in the building. She was quickly losing patience, and I was as ready to give up as I'd ever been. My nerves were fraying more with each passing moment – my legs were shaking and I picked at my fingers, willing the time to move more quickly.

Eventually a female doctor I'd never seen before walked through the door, holding a thick folder of notes. Could all those be about me? She sat on a chair across the room from us.

"What can I do for you today?" she asked, leaning forward as if encouraging me to speak.

Anne squeezed my hand as I gulped and breathed in. "I haven't been doing too well recently. . ." I began. My voice grew a little stronger as I started describing the past couple of months to her. I tried to be as honest as possible, knowing that Anne would jump in if I missed something or tried to hide the truth.

The doctor listened patiently, jotting a few things down as I spoke.

"Are you suicidal?" she asked, looking at me closely.

"No. Not right now. I have been, at times, but not at this moment. I'm feeling too low and empty to be suicidal I think. I think I only feel suicidal when I have a bit more energy to think about it."

"Do you want to come into the hospital here? We can find you a bed if you want to."

"No." It was the only thing I was sure about – my last experience of being in hospital had put me off for good. I knew that I had more chance of getting better with the support of friends and family than in the hospital.

"Okay. What were you expecting by coming here today?"

I didn't know how to answer her. I was only there to appease other people.

Anne leaned forward. "I was the one who persuaded Abbie to come here today because I was worried about her," she explained. "I was hoping you could refer her somewhere, or get some sort of extra outpatient help for her. She sees a psychiatrist here about every six weeks for just a few minutes, and it just isn't enough. Isn't there anything more you can offer her? Therapy groups, or counselling or anything?"

The doctor sat back, chewing her pen and looking thoughtful. "There really isn't anything else we can offer. I'll put in a request for more regular appointments, and see if I can push you up the waiting list to see a psychologist, but other than that, the only other option is coming to stay here for a while until you feel more stable. Which do you want to do?"

I thought about it for a moment, but I knew I didn't want to stay. I couldn't wait to get out of there.

"I don't want to stay – I know that. I guess I'll just go home and keep coming to the psychiatrist as an outpatient."

"You can come back here whenever you want, any hour of the day or night. There'll always be someone here to talk to. Okay?" The doctor looked ready to get back to whatever she'd been doing before. I'd been wasting her time.

"Okay. Thanks." I stood up to go.

Anne stood next to me. I could feel her dissatisfaction. "Is there really nothing else you can do?"

"I'm sorry," the doctor said. "We just don't have the resources to offer anything else. But keep in touch, okay? I'll see if I can get some more things sorted out with the outpatient department. Take care – call us if you need us."

We all walked out of the grey room and went our separate ways.

The rain hit the windscreen in sheets as we drove home. I stared out the window, hypnotized by the rhythmic noise.

"I can't believe that's all they can do!" Anne ranted as she drove. "They should offer more. Don't they realize that inpatient care isn't for everybody? I can't believe we waited for four hours for that! She wasn't even your own doctor!"

I couldn't join in her ranting – I felt nothing but a weighty hopelessness.

"Anne? I need to go home."

"What, now? To your apartment?" Anne sounded apprehensive.

"No, to my parents' house. I think I need to move back home. Is that okay?"

Anne considered it for a moment. "I think it's the best thing to do. But you do realize that you're going to have to tell your mum about the self-harm, don't you? Even if you don't move home permanently, I think she needs to know."

"I don't think I can." The thought of sitting down and being completely truthful with mum was petrifying. After everything, I was still so scared of letting her down.

"Do you agree she needs to know?"

I didn't say anything. I dreaded it, but I realized it was inevitable that she would have to know. Anne seemed to understand my silence.

"Do you want me to tell her?" she asked gently.

"Yes. Please. Is that okay?"

"Of course."

We drove the rest of the way home caught up in our own thoughts.

Both my parents came to the door as soon as we knocked, and I was quickly ushered in from the doorstep. My dad cried, said he was sorry for driving me out and made me feel awkward and embarrassed. The scene epitomized my relationship with my father – somehow he always managed to make himself the center of what was going on. In my heart of hearts I knew he loved me, but I was disgusted that he could only see through his own blinkered view of the world. I felt so little for him that I couldn't see the point in mustering the energy to hug him. My mother sensed all of this and took us into the kitchen, where we sat down with the eternal solution to all problems – a cup of tea.

Anne held my hand under the table, and I stared ahead at the red and yellow tiles on the wall. "Things haven't been great . . ." I began, and then I tailed off, not knowing what to say next. I squeezed Anne's hand.

Mum sat across from me, waiting patiently.

"Abbie's not been coping very well living on her own. She's been finding it very hard to keep eating and has been really depressed. It all came to a head yesterday. She spent last night with Lucy's family and then came to me this morning. We've been at the hospital today, so they know what's been going on, but they don't seem to know what to do. I didn't want her to go back to her apartment and thought you needed to know what was going on." Anne looked at me. "Is that roughly what you wanted to say?"

"Yes," I whispered, refusing to meet my mum's eyes. Mum leaned forward and touched my face.

"I knew things weren't right. You don't tell me things, but I'm your mum – I know on instinct. I would have pushed it with you, but I knew that you were getting support from your friends, and I didn't want to put pressure on you and risk pushing you away. But of course I knew." I saw that her eyes were welling up.

I looked away. "I'm sorry," I whispered. "I feel so guilty for making you worry."

"It's all right. Don't worry about that now. I just want you to be okay. What can I do to make that happen? How can I help?"

"I need to come back home. Is that okay?"

"Of course it is, darling," Mum said gently. "There's always a place for you here – you know that."

We sat in silence for a few moments, staring into the depths of our teacups. I couldn't bear it any longer.

"I'm going to the bathroom," I said. I walked out, hunched over my folded arms. I sat halfway up the stairs to listen.

"There's something else going on that you don't know about, that Abbie's finding really hard to tell you about. It's not just the eating disorder that's a problem for her; she's been struggling with self-harm as well."

There was a short silence before Mum spoke. "I know. I mean, I didn't really know, not definitely, but I suspected." Her voice sounded distant.

"Suspected what?" Anne asked.

"That she'd been hurting herself, cutting and the like. Is that what you're talking about?"

There was a short silence. I assumed Anne was nodding.

"I don't know how I knew really – there are just odd things she's said, and clues here and there. Like going clothes shopping – she suddenly got very private about trying things on, and she'd never been like that before. That was one thing that made me wonder what she was hiding. I pretty much knew for sure when I saw how sympathetic she was during a TV program about it. I didn't want to force it out of her, and I knew she had people like you to talk to. I wish she'd felt able to tell me herself though . . ." Mum's voice tailed off.

Anne spoke softly. "I know it must have been unbearable not pushing her. I don't think I could have done it. You're a very strong woman – stronger than I think I would be. If it helps, she's wanted to tell you for a long time. She just didn't want to give you anything else to worry about."

"To be honest, that's one of the things that worries me. She's so concerned about not worrying me that she won't ask for help. Sometimes she's too considerate for her own good."

"Now you know you can push her more. She knows I've told you – and she wanted me to. I think she would have told you herself, but she doesn't have the words right now. I think what she needs right now is just to be looked after, and not given any decisions to make. As her mum, you're the best person for that."

There were a few moments of silence.

Mum spoke suddenly. "Do you think she's all right? She's been gone a while. Should I go up and find her?"

I jumped up and started back downstairs.

Anne reassured Mum. "I think she's probably been listening to what we've been saying. Abs?" she called out.

I walked back towards the kitchen slowly, ashamed both at my actions and my silence with my mother.

"It's okay, Abs," Mum said. "I don't think any less of you. It'll be fine – we'll do what we need to do. I still love you – I want to help."

I slid back into my place at the table apologetically. "I'm sorry. I wanted to tell you, but I couldn't. I didn't know how."

Mum reached across the table and took my hand. "Don't worry," she reassured me. "We'll work it out. No more secrets, okay?"

I smiled as big a smile as I felt I could manage. "Okay," I whispered.

Both of them smiled at me, each relieved in her own way.

My mum, who knew me better than anyone else in the world, stood up and took my mug.

"Would you like another cup of tea?"

❀　　　❀　　　❀　　　❀

Once I came clean, something snapped in my head and I couldn't face anything at all. I stopped going to work and gave up going to anything where I'd have to talk to people. I didn't want to step outside the door because I might meet someone I knew, but at the same time I didn't want to be at home. Dad was either drunk and yelling or over concerned and suffocating, which made being at home unbearable. He became obsessed with the idea that he was mentally ill because he'd been in a mental health ward. In his gushing moments he talked about how alike we were and he wore "our" afflictions on his sleeve. I loathed the idea of being like my father. So I spent most of my time either shut in my room talking in computer chat rooms, on the yellow sofa at Anne's, or driving randomly around town, listening to music and waiting until I knew Dad would be in bed.

My visit with Anne to the mental health emergency team did accomplish one thing. After three years of being in the mental health system, I finally found myself with a good hospital team. My consultant, Dr. Harvey, was amazing. He took time to listen and understand where I was coming from, and right from the start he put things into place to help me get better. He referred me to other members of the team, and I had a few sessions with a dietician. Although what she said wasn't new to me, she encouraged me no end. I also saw a psychotherapist. Although she didn't like me talking about my faith, I could share things that were bothering me and these appointments gave me something else to put in my schedule. Seeing both the consultant and psychotherapist on a weekly basis gave me two focal points around which I could structure everything else.

I also kept to the structure of the meal rota, partly so that I could relax at home without worrying about food. My relationship with my mum was just beginning to heal and strengthen, and I didn't want arguments over food to get in the way. I made a commitment to Anne, Jayne and Mum that I would eat responsibly, and I took this promise very seriously. Over time, as mealtimes became less stressful for me, I gradually increased the number of meals I was having at home and taking control over. Eventually I just went to Jayne's house on Tuesday evenings – as much to chat and catch up as to eat a meal.

Once I felt that I was on a more even keel I ventured into doing some volunteer work and spent two days a week with a youth work organization. I was careful not to do too much too soon or get into situations where I might be too stressed to keep eating or might feel the need to self-harm. Sometimes I worried that people would think I was lazy for not working full-time, or that I was slacking off and living on benefits to avoid getting a real job. But getting better felt like full-time work to me. I went to bed exhausted every night from fighting the battle against temptation.

Little by little, the days became easier. I joined a choir and started socializing with some other people my age at church. I rediscovered my love of books but, instead of isolating myself in my room, I went out to book discussions and poetry readings at the local library. As I tiptoed back into life again, I realized what I had been missing and began to enjoy myself.

15

"Abbie, I need to talk to you." Mum laid her hand gently on my shoulder.

"Okay." I felt like a teenager, racking my brain to figure out what I'd done wrong.

"We've seen a house," she began. "It's a large cottage with an acre of ground, and it's on the market at a price we can afford."

I sensed a catch was coming. "And . . .?"

"It's in Nottingham, down the road from Grandma and Grandpa." Mum looked at me intently.

I didn't know what to think, much less what to say. I'd assumed our house would always be there – even if I moved out again.

"Everything about it seems perfect," Mum continued. "It means we can get out of London and also look after Grandma and Grandpa. And it would be a new start for Dad. I think he needs that. You'd be the only reason to stay. I know that's a big load to put on you, but we really think this is the right move right now."

I couldn't help thinking about myself. "Where am I going to go?"

"It's up to you. There'll always be a place for you with us, you know that, but if you want to stay in this area, we'll find you somewhere else. Why don't you think about it for a while and we can talk more about it later."

It wasn't an easy decision. Staying with mum and dad felt safe, and I was very aware that every other time I'd left home I hadn't been able to cope. But I couldn't imagine leaving the town I'd grown up in, my hospital team and the support network I'd built up. Could I risk moving out on my own again so I wouldn't have to leave the life I was beginning to build for myself and the church and friends who had given me so much?

Eventually, knowing that I could always move to Nottingham later if things didn't work out, I decided to stay. I moved into the spare room of a family friend who was looking for a lodger, and started, once again, trying to live independently from my parents. The transition was difficult, but I kept my head above water. Living with Carol and her two boys meant that I still had the structure of family life available to me if I wanted.

One of the main advantages of living on my own was that I began to make friends my own age, rather than just spending time with those who had acted like parents towards me. My friendships with Jayne and Anne were very important to me, but they weren't the peer relationships that I longed for. As I grew in confidence and was therefore able to be more sociable, I became a quarter of a close friendship group with three other women from church. I had never had friends like Michelle, Caroline and Allison, and I loved spending time with them and sharing in their lives. For the first time I felt like I was in give-and-take relationships – not just with one good friend, but three. I trusted them, and I knew they trusted me.

As time went on I spent more and more time with them, especially Michelle, whose two young boys I loved more than any other children I'd known, and whose husband always made me welcome. Michelle, Caroline and Allison all knew my history, but I also knew their stories, and we bonded in a way that was completely new to me. We shared our struggles, prayed together, drank many cups of tea and coffee, and talked for hours as our friendships deepened. As I spent more time confiding in them and they in me, my hospital appointments became less and less necessary as I became more adept at communicating what I was feeling. I didn't need structure as much, or to control my eating, and as I gained control over other aspects of everyday life I didn't feel the need to self-harm either. I finally felt like I was on the road to being a normal woman, and I relished every minute of it.

I thought that part of living a normal life was living alone. I wanted to experience living like other people my age. So, through contacts at church, I found two housemates and an apartment to rent. The other bit of normality I was desperate for was a job – a career in which I could feel of some use. Although I had started a degree, and done some work in retail, I wasn't really qualified for anything. So part of rebuilding my life was deciding what I was going to do. I wanted to help people who were finding life difficult, and I considered everything from social work to nursing to youth work. Eventually, I decided to train as a counsellor. I was interested in how people dealt with the problems life threw at them, and I wanted to help those in recovery, learning from the ways I'd been both helped and hindered.

I found a course run by London Bible College one day a week – it seemed sensible not to jump straight into full-time study when I'd been out of action for so long, and I wanted to make sure I still had time to stay in contact with all the people who'd been supporting me. As I continued my own journey to recovery, I realized that the most dangerous times for me came when I isolated myself, and I was determined that I wasn't going to put myself in that position. My application to do the course was accepted, and I waited restlessly for the first day as I devoured the required reading list. I knew I was going to love it.

❀   ❀   ❀   ❀

As I stepped into the classroom on the first day, I began to doubt myself again. There were so many people! When I arrived there were already about forty people waiting for the first lecture to start. Many of them seemed to know each other already and I felt alone in the crowd. As I looked around I realized that I was one of the younger people in the class. I was sure everyone else had far more knowledge and experience than I'd ever have.

I found an empty seat and sank down, already tired from driving an unfamiliar route in rush hour. I started flicking self-consciously through the folder that was on each table.

"Is it alright if I sit here?" a voice behind me asked.

I turned around to see a blonde girl, about my age, with a lovely smile.

I nodded and smiled, relieved not to be sitting on my own anymore.

"I'm Samantha – Sam."

"I'm Abbie. Can you believe how crazy this is? It's manic!"

"I know – I love it. Have you been here before? Where are you from?"

"I live about 20 miles away. It isn't far, but it seems like forever when you have to battle the traffic. And no, I've never been here before. It's a bit overwhelming. Where are you from?"

"Paraguay. It's a long story!" she smiled.

As Sam and I chatted I found out that she was a missionary, using her furlough year to study counselling. I listened in amazement as she told me her exciting life story.

We were interrupted by a soft voice beside us. "Can I join you? I don't know anyone."

"Neither did we until five minutes ago!" Sam beamed, gesturing to the tall dark girl, who introduced herself as Clare, to sit with us.

When the instructor told us that our first topic of study would be the history of counselling I smiled. I knew I was going to love it.

Each Wednesday, after a morning chapel service, we had a full day of lectures and meals together. We also had structured time to practice counselling skills and techniques in groups of three. We were to use issues from our own lives, and Sam, Clare and I worked together as a group. I found it all fascinating – the counselling model itself and how to use it, as well as learning about the history of counselling and pastoral care, different types of secular and Christian counselling, human growth and development and ethics.

We learned a counselling model based on the concept that God created everyone to be in a perfect relationship with him. Before the fall, Adam and Eve's deepest needs – to feel secure, significant and of worth – were met in God so perfectly that they didn't even realize they had these needs. By disobeying God and believing the lies of the serpent, who told them they could be as powerful as God, Adam and Eve forged for us an inheritance of trying to meet our needs outside of God. The root of human struggles is our striving to meet our needs in things other than the love of God. When we wrongly believe, consciously or not, that things of the world can meet our needs, we experience negative emotions. Correcting these wrong beliefs and seeking God to fulfill our needs instead can reverse many of the emotions and issues with which we struggle.

As I saw this model of counselling at work within our group, I began to see how true this was in my own life. As I looked back over the years I recognized the ways in which I'd tried to meet my own deepest needs rather than relying on God to meet them. I could see that longing in myself – to feel significant, to be secure in people's love and to know that I was of worth to others. I made the powerful discovery that the only way to know and feel these things perfectly is through the love of God, accepting that he is the only one who is faultless and who will never fail me.

The sessions with my triplet were very therapeutic for me. Although I had worked through many issues and had been determined to go to college with a wonderful testimony of healing, as I talked through different situations with Sam and Clare I saw that I wasn't the 100% healthy person that I claimed to be. I had dealt with a lot of the surface problems and changed my behavior, but I was still just as flawed underneath as I had been in the midst of my self-harming. I began to search my past and present feelings to discover the ineffective ways that I tried to meet those needs. I sought to be objective, to acknowledge my tendencies to rely on people and things instead of on God, and to see the changes I still needed to make.

By examining my reasons for turning to self-destruction in the first place, I discovered a lot about my personality and the way I deal with things. I realized there were deeper issues that I still hadn't addressed and that I was tempted to leave hidden. I still had a lot to learn about coping with the things that life threw at me, and I was in for some surprises as I began to look below the surface to see the ways in which God was longing to change me. It was hard to dredge up those things, but it was better to deal with them than to wait for them to creep up on me and affect my eating or cause me to self-harm again. Because Helena had also studied counseling here before starting Kainos, a lot of what I was studying cemented what she'd taught me. Since I was able to apply the theory to my own life, I understood the material in a deeper way than I might have otherwise. Hours spent talking with Sam and Clare highlighted some of the behaviors and thought patterns I still had to change in my life.

❀   ❀   ❀   ❀

"Guys? Can I ask you something?"

Sam, Clare and I were sitting in the field, eating our packed lunches in the blazing spring sunshine. They both looked up and nodded, mouths full.

"Do you think I'm a perfectionist?"

Sam snorted and Clare, who was having problems keeping her sandwich in her mouth, whacked her on the back. They both looked at me and dissolved into giggles.

"What's so funny? I'm serious!" I was indignant.

"No Abs, you're not a perfectionist," said Clare.

I felt hopeful.

"I mean, you retype all your notes when you get home, and color-code them, and you stress if you can't find your hole-punch or stapler . . ."

Sam joined in, ". . . and you line up all your pens before every lecture and freak out if you lose a lid . . ."

". . . and I think you probably polish your folder as soon as you get home . . ."

". . . but no, you're not a perfectionist!"

I couldn't decide whether to laugh with them or punch them. "Is it annoying? Hey, I'm serious!"

The girls tried to sober up.

"It's just that I was wondering. Just because I've given up controlling my eating and self-harm, maybe I'm still making unhealthy decisions to feel okay. And I don't know why being a perfectionist should make me feel better, but it does. Is that crazy?"

Clare looked to Sam, who tried to answer. "You are a perfectionist, Abs, but that's not necessarily something to worry about. What you need to ask yourself is what it does for you. Why does it make you feel better? What needs that are met by being a perfectionist are unhealthy for you?"

"I'm not sure," I began. "I guess I hide behind it. I like to look like I'm completely organized so that people think I'm a good student, and that I know what I'm doing. If I look clever, I might fool people into thinking that I actually am. I guess I'm scared of people thinking I can't do things. Does that make sense?"

Sam looked thoughtful. "I think so. So it's weakness you're afraid of? Not being as good as other people?"

"Yes. I'm so scared of people picking out my weak points that I try to do things they make positive comments about. If I'm super-organized I get praised – if I wasn't they might see that I'm actually a useless student and criticize me. I couldn't cope with that."

"What's so bad about criticism?" Clare asked, leaning into the conversation.

"I guess I don't want people to think I'm inadequate or that I don't belong here. I can't bear the idea of being judged – even constructive criticism is hard to hear, because it means that what I've done is no good." The words sounded true as they came out of my mouth, but I felt a little surprised that I was able articulate this feeling that had been gnawing at me for a while.

"I think I see what you're getting at. Doing something less than perfectly somehow makes you a bad person.

That's why you set yourself such high standards, so you can feel like a 'good' person." Sam wiggled her fingers to enclose the word "good" in air quotes. "Your self-esteem really isn't good is it – it's like you can pick out a negative comment at twenty paces! Is that why you criticize yourself so often, so other people can't?"

"Yes, partly," I admitted. "And also – this is horrible – I know if I criticize myself, other people will say good things to make me feel better." As I spoke, the ugliness of how I manipulated people suddenly hit me. "Isn't that awful?"

Sam tried to comfort me. "I think everyone does that to some extent, Abbie. You're just being honest about it."

"You know," I continued, "I've been so caught up thinking that doing something badly meant that I was a bad person that I've been trying to live life proving I'm not. That impossible goal of being perfect drives everything I do. And it's so… so self-focused." I felt embarrassed and stupid. "That's one of those wrong beliefs we've been talking about. How am I ever going to change the way I think about everything?" I sank down onto the grass. I hadn't felt that hopeless in quite awhile.

"Maybe what you need to change is the way you think about weakness," Clare suggested gently. "You think about it as a huge fault, but maybe it isn't. The Bible says that God's power is made perfect in weakness. He can show his power in us much more when we're weak and relying on him than he can when we're battling the world on our own, determined to be strong."

Sam had been flicking through her Bible. "Second Corinthians twelve, verse ten," she informed me, sticking the Bible right under my nose and giggling when I couldn't focus on it properly.

Clare carried on seriously. "And the other thing is, if you're good at everything and have no weakness, it makes other people uncomfortable. Being a perfectionist can make you unapproachable because people don't think they can live up to your standards. If you don't accept weakness in yourself, how do you think other people are going to feel about sharing their weaknesses with you in counselling?"

As I drove home that evening, I couldn't stop thinking about what Clare had said. I'd been studying these deep human needs, but how was I meeting my own needs for self-worth, significance and security?

Self-worth, I realized, was an easy one. I'd perfected the art of inviting affirmation from other people rather than seeking affirmation in the word of God and my knowledge of his love for me. The other scary thought that hit me was that I lived my life in terror of doing something wrong. If I didn't deal with this, I realized, I would lead a rigid and increasingly closed-off life.

All I had to do to feel significant was to do everything, and do it perfectly. I looked for opportunities to do things that other people would affirm me for – like Clare and Sam's examples of my ultra-organization. I was desperate to find something that I alone was good at so that I could feel significant. Besides setting a path for self-destruction, seeking significance in perfectionism blinded me to how significant I am in God's eyes.

And how did I meet my need for security? I surrounded myself with people so I never had to be alone. But the sad irony is that I couldn't open up to these people in case they found out what a bad person I was and left me, which would only serve to confirm what a bad person I was. So I was never truly secure in other people because my relationships depended on them not really knowing me. It never occurred to me to look to God for security, in whose eyes I was created perfectly.

After all the years of self-loathing, it was difficult to accept and live out these truths. The whole year at London Bible College was like that – every time I thought I had it all figured out, another wrong belief, or something else from my past, reared its ugly head. I wasn't alone – all the students began to look differently at their own lives. I finally realized that the distinction I had made between myself and others was entirely inaccurate – it just wasn't true that everyone else was fine and I was useless. I was amazed that God actually used me to support and comfort other people who were struggling through that year. Through doing this I was able to see outside of my own worldview and was forced to accept my own weakness as I would anyone else's.

As the course drew to an end, I was able to see how my life had changed in the space of just a year. I had started the course thinking, naively, that I had come through everything life had to throw at me – that I was out the other side, ready to start helping other people. Through learning more about how I was created, I finally came to the realization that I would never be fully at the end of the road on this side of eternity. God would always be doing work in me as long as I was willing to let him.

During our final session together, Sam, Clare and I had a great discussion about what we had learned through the year. They each shared their high point, but when it was my turn I wasn't sure how to choose just one. When I realized which lesson had set most of the others in motion, I was a little surprised myself.

"I think the most important lecture for me was the one about forgiveness. Do you remember? We were discussing how important forgiveness is in the counselling process – not just the client being forgiven by God, but also the process of forgiving other people, forgiving God, and forgiving themselves. It really hit me then how much unforgiveness I'd been holding on to. I was better in terms of the eating and self-harm, but it wasn't until I forgave people that I actually felt free of the past. It meant that I could accept why I went through what I did."

Sam leaned forward. "Can you explain? How did forgiving help you understand things from the past?"

"Because," I continued, "once I'd forgiven people for the things they did, I could start to think about the events in a rational way and see how they shaped me. Like when I was a kid. My thinking was skewed by the way I wrongly interpreted things my parents and my brother said, but I couldn't think about it all properly because the memories were too painful. Once I had forgiven them, I could think more clearly about how I took their comments. I finally understood that they never meant to be hurtful. But I couldn't make sense of it or understand how it affected me until I forgave them and got rid of the bitterness."

"I think I see," Sam said, "but what about your dad? Have you been able to forgive him for all the things he's said?"

"That was harder," I admitted. "Forgiving him was much more an act of will that an emotional decision, and I don't think I've finished the process of forgiveness there. But being willing to forgive him meant that I could put some of my anger aside and recognize that he has his own struggles. I also realized that he isn't the only one responsible for the barrier between us. I have to take some responsibility for it, too. Forgiving people kind of commits you to rebuilding relationships!"

"What about forgiving yourself?" Clare asked. "Does forgiving others mean that you're more aware of being forgiven by God?"

"Accepting forgiveness from God has been a long process for me," I said. "I knew that he had forgiven me, but it didn't feel real until I accepted it. Accepting God's forgiveness meant that I could then forgive myself for the wrong choices I'd made. And that enables me to rely on him more, which I finally understand isn't an act of weakness – it's how I was created."

"You've had an amazing year, haven't you?" Clare said. "It seems like you've learned loads."

"And you've certainly grown in confidence since last September," Sam added. Clare nodded in agreement.

"So," I asked, "what's next?"

"That's easy for me," said Sam. "I fly back to Paraguay in four weeks!"

"And I just go back to my job," Clare shrugged. "I'm sure I'll use all the things I've learned, but I don't know that my life will be hugely different. What about you, Abbie?"

"I have no idea," I smiled. "But I'm looking forward to finding out."

At our graduation ceremony the following week I smiled as I watched my classmates walk forward to collect their certificates. I thanked God for the friends I'd made and the many things I'd learned from them. As I heard my name and walked up to the stage, a feeling of pride welled up in me – I had finally finished something without having to drop out. I basked in this celebration of our accomplishment. I was ready to take on the world.

16

Then I had a blip.

Only a few weeks after finishing the course I was missing the friends I'd made, the challenge of studying and having a purpose to focus on. I knew I wasn't ready to counsel other people, but I didn't know what else I could do. Having done something I enjoyed so wholeheartedly, I didn't want to do a job that didn't interest me. But nothing seemed to interest me. I spent the summer doing very little, stuck in a rut of not knowing what to do next.

By September I was sinking fast from sadness into depression. I began to suppress my feelings, which also meant that I began to deal with and express them in other ways. There was no conscious decision this time – I fought against everything negative, but I felt swamped by the negative feelings. My weight began to drop as I struggled to eat healthy amounts. Every time I had a meal I panicked and felt unable to cope, so I made myself sick. I began every meal determined that it would be fine, but I always ended up on my knees in front of the toilet. Every day I swore it was the last time, but I always found myself back there, hating myself for being weak and giving in. The autumn got colder as my eating disorder regained control, and eventually I couldn't hide it any more.

❀ ❀ ❀ ❀

It was almost midnight and Michelle and I were at Caroline's, where we had gone for coffee after the evening church service. God had touched each of us during the service, and we were determined not to let what he had said slide. We sat in the dim light of Caroline's back room, discussing what was happening in our lives and putting together plans to make our lives more God-focused. We sealed our agreement to meet to pray and study the Bible more often with caffeine, shortbread and light-hearted chat.

"So," Caroline filled a pause in the conversation and turned to look at me. "Are we going to talk about the food thing?"

I didn't know what to say. "The food thing?" I repeated, feeling like a naughty schoolgirl who'd been found out. I looked at Michelle, trying to figure out which side she was on.

"It's kind of obvious, Abs," Michelle said.

"Okay, okay, things haven't been great in that department – but I've got it under control, I really have," I stumbled defensively. I could taste the saltiness of the lies in the back of my throat.

"How much weight have you actually lost?" Caroline asked.

"Only a bit. I don't know, but it can't be much. I don't look any different and my clothes still fit." I was telling the truth – I didn't think I looked any different.

"Abs, if we can tell you've lost weight then you must have lost quite a bit. You're looking way too thin. And your clothes are too big, look." Michelle pulled at the loose waistband of my jeans.

We sat in silence for a while. I was thinking of some of the things I'd put Anne and Jayne through when I was at my worst. The last thing I wanted to do was risk hurting or worrying my new friends in that way.

"When did it start?" Caroline finally asked.

"Over the summer. I was miserable after college finished. I didn't know what to do with myself. I didn't really notice it at first, but then it started to get the better of me. Before I knew it I was feeling really low again and dealing with it the only way I knew how." I paused. "It's gotten steadily worse," I admitted. I wanted to be as truthful as possible with them.

"Are you eating at all?" Caroline asked.

"Kind of. I guess I'm limiting my intake a bit, but I am trying to keep something in me – otherwise I get so tired. And I know that if I don't eat anything at all, it's harder to start again."

"Are you throwing up?"

I stared down at my hands and nodded.

"Running a lot?"

Another nod.

"Cutting?"

"A bit. Nothing like before. Just to keep me going." I looked up at them with tears in my eyes. "I'm so sorry. Are you disappointed in me?"

"Not disappointed. Concerned, maybe, and a little helpless, but not disappointed," Caroline said gently.

"Why didn't you tell us? If you were feeling that bad, why didn't you say something?" Michelle looked troubled.

"Because it's hard to admit to. I didn't want to be 'anorexic Abbie' any more. I wanted to be grown-up, fully-functioning, counsellor Abbie, who'd sorted her life out and moved on. I feel like I've got my life back – when people see me they see someone who's capable of doing something, who's achieved things. I didn't want to go back to being seen as helpless. People look up to me now, they ask my advice about things. I don't want to lose that. I was just going to handle it myself." Even as I spoke I could hear the counsellor in me. *"And where are you getting your significance and self-worth now, Abbie?"* The other voice in my head whispered a sharp jab of truth that burst my self-inflated coping bubble.

Michelle took my hand. "The thing is, Abs, you're not handling it. Are you?"

My two best friends sat looking at me, waiting for my answer.

"No. I'm not," I admitted.

A week later, I moved into Michelle's guest room. Everything had gone downhill so quickly that I felt a constant and intense emotional exhaustion. Was I really back in the depths again? I wanted to talk it all through, to find some solutions and work towards them, but I simply could not. I had no energy, no spark of ingenuity or enthusiasm. I was so worn out that I just wanted to wash my hands of it.

I knew how much hard work I'd have to put into getting better, because I'd done it before. If only I could pour what was left of me into someone else's hands and have them do it all for me. I yearned for someone to come along and say something amazing, to which I could respond, "Yes! That's it! That's what I need to do!" In the past it had worked, and I'd pulled myself together and started to live again. I wrote in my journal:

> So why are the old solutions not enough now? Am I really as proud as to say "been there, done that" and never again make the effort? It would appear so. . . .

> It sounds petulant to say that I've done my share of hard work and I don't want to do it anymore, but that's how I feel. I don't want to bother any more, I just want to curl up in a corner and cease to be. Just stop being. Give up.

Suicidal? No, not really. If life were just slightly easier, if I could see just a fraction of light at the end of the tunnel, I'd want to do life, to carry on being part of it. But it all feels like one hard slog, with no way of ever being different, just an endless struggle to stay on an even keel, pairing the good with the bad just to stay alive in the battle with the monster I feel lives inside me, just waiting to devour me. And I know I should be able to see a way out, because there's been a time when things have been better, but "should" doesn't come into it. I can't see it. Not because I'm not trying – I just can't. It's like there's a wall around this moment in time, and I can't see over it.

The thing is, I should be fine because I know there's hope, I know there's peace to be had, I know there's joy in life. I should be able to see the light at the end of the tunnel because I know that Christ is the light of the world. I'm parading myself around as a Christian, but I'm not living as one, and I feel like I'm living a lie.

And here was the heart of my struggle: I finally felt that I looked like a good Christian. For the first time ever I was able to lead in some ways. People had begun to look up to me. They were impressed that I'd been to Bible college. I had been given responsibilities at church, leading worship and preaching occasionally. I was a Kainos success story, and I had shared my testimony of healing from an eating disorder and self-harm on various occasions. But with the eating disorder creeping up behind me again, I knew I was losing my grip on the life I wanted to live for God.

I thought of myself as selfish, proud, and self-centered. These seemed to be the right words to explain my dislike of myself, but as the eating disorder and self-harm took hold again I saw the truth of this description in a deeper and more terrifying way. Instead of taking these thoughts to God, repenting, trying to change and living in humility, I remained in this frame of mind. I berated myself constantly for being a bad Christian and stayed in my eating disorder. But I saw God more accurately than I ever had. One night, after a long walk, I wrote the following letter to God:

> Where are you? You promised you'd always be here, and now, when I need you, I'm looking everywhere and you're nowhere to be found. I feel desolate, lost, without direction, completely alone. I've been walking around in circles, wondering if you're hidden in a bit of ground I've not yet covered, but now my legs are weak and the pain is too much for me.

> Can't you see the pain I'm in? Now is when I need you! I know you choose to be silent sometimes, but you certainly pick your moments.

> This is too much for me. I cannot do this alone. I need help, and I know that yours is the only help that will be any good. You are the only one I can reach out to – there is none like you – this I know above all things. You are everything I need; all I ever wished for or desired I can find in you. All of what I know about you makes you worthy to be praised, and that's what I pledge to you. I will praise you for as long as my ordained time on earth lasts. And when that ends I will praise you in heaven.

> But my praise for you doesn't mean I feel you near. You feel so far away. I know how little I deserve to have you near, and I know I am unworthy to come anywhere close to you.

But you promised! And I feel like you're not following through. I know you must be close by, because I believe what you've said to me in your word, and will never refute that. But I want to feel you. Now.

I just want not to feel alone. For just a minute I want not to feel anxious, or depressed, or frustrated, or lonely, or like giving up, or guilty, or ashamed. Is that too much to ask? I know you died for my sin, but I feel like I'm carrying it around on my back where it weighs me down and inside where it threatens to explode. I don't know how to get it out except through you, but you are somewhere I can't reach. I know it must be me and not you, Lord, but please just help me now. I need you. I can't do this without you.

I was desperate not to be like this. This time I knew that something else was possible. Every other time I had been this low I had thought it was the only way to live – I couldn't imagine coping without self-harming and controlling my eating. This time was different. I had tasted recovery, delighted in it and wanted with every fiber of my being to stay healthy. But it felt like the old monsters were devouring me from the inside out, and there wasn't much left.

Life with Michelle's young family provided plenty of distractions to help me get through each day. I spent a lot of my time playing with her two pre-school-age sons. I dreaded mealtimes, and especially the evening meal, but I learned to face each meal as a necessary hardship – horrid at the time, but helpful in the long run. Michelle was a great cook, and I felt that I was letting her down by not eating. I knew she was watching me, making sure I didn't hide food or sneak to the bathroom afterwards. I hated this but knew it was necessary, both for my own well-being and so she wouldn't worry as much.

The evenings, after the kids were in bed, were excruciating. I sat with Michelle and her husband in front of the television, trying to concentrate and laughing when they laughed – but I was constantly battling with the clamor in my head that demanded I cut or binge. Most nights it was sheer willpower that kept me sitting there.

Bedtime was a welcome relief, as I could finally relax and take off my tired coping face. I could cry and write and bleed some of the feelings into my journal. I tried not to cut – although I didn't always manage. Bingeing was impossible as their sleeping Labrador stood unwitting guard in the kitchen. Thoughts of worthlessness and hopelessness plagued me as I tossed and turned. In the darkness it seemed impossible that I would ever feel better again, and my thoughts would unravel into senseless jibes at myself until I was too worn out to stay awake and drifted into nightmares of food and fat and razorblades.

And then it was morning, and the whole cycle began again. As each day dragged by, I got closer and closer to giving up.

❀   ❀   ❀   ❀

"Are you sure you don't mind?" Michelle asked for the fourth time as her husband dragged her toward the door.

"Of course I don't. Anyway, they're asleep. It's not exactly the hardest babysitting job I've ever done. Go, have fun!"

"And you're sure you'll be okay?"

"I'm sure. You're only going to the club for a swim. I'll be fine, don't worry about me. I'll be okay."

"Alright, if you're sure. We'll be back by nine. Phone Caroline if you need anything. Or if you get lonely. Phone her anyway, okay?" Michelle's voice tailed off as she was dragged towards her car.

Reassuring as I tried to be, I could understand her worry – she hadn't left me on my own since I'd moved in with them.

I wandered back into the front room and switched on the television, flicking through the channels to find something vaguely interesting. Twenty minutes later, I realized that I'd missed the whole show. I didn't know what I'd been thinking, or why I couldn't remember, but all of a sudden I felt a weight on my shoulders, pressing down so I could hardly breathe. Panic attacks always seem to come at the most inopportune times. I knew I couldn't have picked a worse time to space out, and yet it wasn't in my control. I struggled to keep myself tethered to reality.

Had I been able to think straight, it might have been easier to see the way through and out the other side. But I couldn't see past nine o'clock that evening, when I would no longer be alone in the house. As I watched the clock, 8:35 rolled into 8:36 and took far too long over it. Although I was very aware of my responsibility for the boys, who were sound asleep upstairs, I didn't think I was going to make it to nine o'clock. I had nothing left in me to fight.

Everything seemed so black that I couldn't see clearly. The despair in my heart literally clouded my vision, and I bumped into things as I collected what I needed to get myself back into one piece.

I sat in the dim light of the conservatory, razor and vein laid open before me. By that point I didn't care how much blood flowed, or whether I would be able to stop it. I just needed to feel better. I tried to look back over my life, so it would flash before my eyes as all dramatic literature says it's supposed to, but there was nothing. I started to cut along the most visible blood vessel of my wrist, desperate to get something to spill and release the pressure.

And yet, for some reason, the blood didn't flow. Despite being a pro at self-harm and knowing that veins hold blood that moves through the body, I couldn't get my arm to bleed. I didn't understand what was happening. Why wasn't it working? I didn't even care if it all went too far and I died – I just needed to bleed, to feel the pain that I knew would bring me back to the world in some semblance of wholeness. I pushed at the blood vessel, pumped my hand and tried cutting again, going deeper into my wrist, but nothing happened. It was as if there was no blood in my body. I sat and stared into the darkness, perturbed and exhausted.

The phone cut into my thoughts.

It turned out to be a wrong number, but reality kicked in. I phoned Jayne and she came over. She was still there when Michelle came back from her swim. I saw her face fall as she realized what had happened – the promise I'd made not to cut had disintegrated like so many before.

The rest of the evening passed in a blur. Jayne and Michelle talked to each other, and I nodded and agreed cooperatively. I was so confused. I wasn't sure what had happened. I tried to answer for myself, I tried to laugh things off, I tried crying, I tried cracking jokes, I tried drinking wine. Nothing worked, and I went to bed feeling like a complete failure, hoping that I'd never wake up.

17

The next day, sitting at the breakfast table, it dawned on me.

"Michelle? I just realized something. I was infuriated last night. That might not sound good, but it is, because it means that I felt something. I thought I had come to the point where I couldn't feel any emotion, but I don't think that's true. So, if I felt infuriated, I might also be able to feel good sometime. I know it probably sounds obvious and a bit weird, but that actually gives me hope."

"That sounds like an important realization." Michelle was serious.

"It is. When I'm panicking later, can you remind me what I just said?"

"So, do you think you're ready to make some changes?" she asked.

I leaned my elbows on the table. "I don't know. It sounds really hard, and I know it is but I also know, somehow, that it will be worth it. I think last night gave me some of my hope back. It's as if there's a switch in my head, and now that it's turned on I've suddenly realized what everyone else knew all along." I paused and looked Michelle in the eye as I let the truth sink in myself. "I don't have to do this."

Michelle didn't answer. We just smiled, sharing in a moment that we both knew was profound.

❀   ❀   ❀   ❀

"So," said Lucy as she stirred the enormous mug of coffee she'd just bought, "do you think it was God who made it so you didn't bleed? Do you think that was his way of telling you it was time to sort things out?" She licked the froth off her stirrer and twiddled it in her fingers.

"Maybe. I haven't figured out how it could have happened – it really should have bled a lot. It doesn't make sense any other way. Kind of extreme, though, don't you think?" I tried to smile.

"You obviously weren't listening properly – I don't think that would have been God's first choice for getting your attention! He obviously had to give you a big kick up the backside to make you notice!"

I flicked foam at her from the top of my coffee. "The truth is, I did know those things. I guess I just needed to be reminded. But I know I have to rely on God, and I know I have to use the strength he's given me and not try to do it on my own. And I know that I have to accept that people love me and care for me and want me to be well, and that's hard sometimes. When I think about how I've treated some people, I can't imagine why on earth they'd still want to be around me, let alone help me."

"So what now? What do you think God's telling you to do with your life?"

"I have no idea. Because he intervened so drastically I think he has a plan for me, but at the moment I can't think beyond trying to make healthy decisions each minute of the day. Know what I mean?"

"Of course I do – I'm still on that road myself. It's amazing when you think of what we were like a few years ago when we first met. You were so quiet, you hardly spoke!" Lucy smiled.

"And you were so cold all the time from not eating that you lived in a fleece when the rest of us were in t-shirts!"

We giggled at the memory.

Lucy's face grew serious. "But if you'd told me back then that in four years I would be practically recovered and working as a nurse, I'd never have believed you. And you probably wouldn't have believed where you'd be, either."

"I wouldn't. I know we used to laugh when Helena said it's a process, but it's true – although I'm not sure I would have wanted to know back then how long a process it is! But I can see how things have changed for each of us over time. And we're much closer to being free now than we were back then." I sat back. Now that I stopped to think, there were a lot of things that Helena had said that were finally working in my life.

"You know what's different, though?" Lucy mused. "Now, I can't wait for the next step in the process. Life is so exciting – I can't wait to see where it goes next."

❀   ❀   ❀   ❀

"How are you doing?" Michelle sat across the table, pretending she hadn't been watching me battle with a bowl of cereal.

"Okay. I'm nearly there. I know it takes me a long time, but asking me every five minutes isn't going to speed it up."

I shot her a sly smile.

"Well, at least you're getting your sense of humor back," she laughed as she swatted me playfully with a towel.

I grinned. "Maybe I am. Or maybe I just like seeing you squirm."

"I'm serious, Abs. That's the first time I've heard you crack a joke in weeks. I'm not pretending everything's fine and dandy just because you made fun of me, but you do seem to be doing better. How is everything really?"

I frowned. "It's not easy. Sometimes I think about giving up on it all. But then I just have to remind myself that it's worth it. And it helps being here – I can look at the boys having fun, or at you and Andy and the relationship you have, and all of that helps me believe that things can be better. It's all about telling myself the right things."

"I'm glad you're getting some of your perspective back. There was a time not long ago when I thought you'd lost it permanently. It was like you couldn't see the future at all, or the effect you had on anyone else. It was so unlike you."

"I know. It's one of the things I feel really badly about. I just couldn't see past trying anything to feel better, whatever the cost to my health or anyone else's well-being. I'm sorry. I know it doesn't change anything, but I really mean it."

"It's okay, really it is," Michelle reached her hand across the table to me. "I'm not going to pretend that it wasn't difficult, or that I didn't feel hurt sometimes, but that was the eating disorder talking, not you. I just had to keep reminding myself that it wasn't really you, and that you were just my friend stuck in a cage that did all your talking and acting for you."

"Thank you for understanding and persevering. In case I haven't said it before, I can't tell you how much I appreciate it."

"You have said it before – many times – but I'll listen to it again!" Michelle smiled and pushed her chair back. "So, what do you want to do now?"

"You're probably going to think it's crazy, but I want to go home."

Michelle froze.

"I know I haven't got everything sorted out yet," I continued, "but I need to get my life back. I know I'm living much better, but I'm living your life, not mine. I spend my days doing whatever you do, and that's not real. I need to get back to doing what I do. Does that make sense?"

She sat back down, looking thoughtful. "It does make sense. It worries me, but I think you're right. You need to figure out how to get through each day on your own. But I think we need to make a plan, like the going-home plan you did at Kainos. Maybe we could come up with some goals for how you're going to carry on getting better, and then how you're going to stay well."

I nodded and she got up to get some paper and a pen.

"Okay," she said as she sat back down, "if we plan everything to start with – mealtimes, relaxing times, and everything, then you can cut things out as you feel stronger. And you have to promise you'll talk to someone if things get even a tiny bit out of hand – me, Caroline, Allison, Anne, Jayne – someone."

"I will. Thanks for understanding."

❁   ❁   ❁   ❁

I looked up at the house. I had finished packing my car and was ready to go. I felt a strong urge to run back inside and stay forever. But I also knew it was time to go home and live on my own again. Michelle stood beside me anxiously.

"Phone me when you get in?"

"I promise."

"And we'll see you for dinner later?"

"I'll be back at six, ready to be stuffed full of all the goodies you prepare. It's only four hours away – I can be on my own for four hours! Please, don't worry. I'll be fine."

"Okay. See you later." She turned and hugged me.

I couldn't breathe very well, but I didn't mind – it felt good to be alive.

As she released me, she pushed my hair back from my face. "I'm proud of you, you know that?"

❀   ❀   ❀   ❀

Although I was ready and exhilarated to be living my life again, going home was not without its challenges. I had to relearn how to do things that had always been part of my routine and I needed my friends for practical things far more than I thought I would. On my first visit to the grocery store I had to phone Michelle, who came to rescue me from cowering in the cereal aisle because I couldn't make any decisions about what food to buy. Caroline had even more opportunities to practice patience when a quick trip shopping for black trousers took four hours. And when some old friends from college invited me out for dinner, I had to go on a test run to the restaurant with Michelle, Caroline and Allison first, so that I would know what to order and what it would look like when it arrived.

It took time, but I slowly regained my strength and independence. I forced myself to make decisions and try new things, and I used the willpower I'd formerly turned towards self-destruction in a far more positive way. I made extra efforts not to be isolated and stayed in contact with friends who would always ask me how things were going.

About six weeks after moving back home I met John. We were introduced at church – and suddenly he seemed to appear wherever I went. He was tall and blonde, with an open mind and a quirky sense of humor, and I felt the attraction immediately. Unfortunately, I also felt the panic. I was still so vulnerable.

I pestered Michelle with my questions. "Am I really ready for a relationship? Isn't it too soon? I'm only just getting back on track – would I be stupid to introduce someone else into the equation? He's lovely, but what if he doesn't understand? What if he gets to know me and realizes he hates me?"

Michelle didn't have the answers, and I'm not sure John would have either if I'd had the courage to ask him. But I didn't really have the chance to think it through logically. When we didn't arrange to meet we'd bump into each other – in town, at the gym, at someone's house after church. We began dating before we really knew what was happening, and I found myself in a serious relationship. I told him things I thought I'd never be able to voice, and I found it easy to share with him that I was still sorting through things in my head.

One night, when we were sitting on his sofa sharing memories of our childhoods, he showed me a scar on his knee from a long-ago argument with his brother and a bicycle.

I swallowed my fear and said softly, "I have some scars to show you, too." I held my breath and lifted my t-shirt a couple of inches, showing the raised zig-zags on my abdomen.

He traced them with his finger and then leaned over and kissed the tip of my nose. "It's like a map," he said. "It shows the roads you've been down."

I let out my breath in a single sigh of relief and snuggled into him. From that point onwards I was certain I wanted to be with him the rest of my life, and five months later we were engaged to be married.

❋　　　❋　　　❋　　　❋

Our wedding day went by in a dream. The June weather was warm and sunny but not too hot, and I felt as elated as I ever had. I had the perfect dress, the perfect shoes and the perfect flowers, and I felt beautiful. My conscientious bridesmaids, Lucy and Michelle, thwarted my attempts to phone John every five minutes as the hour grew closer. They busied themselves with make-up and hair. We sipped champagne with the photographer, who took pictures against the backdrop of Michelle's garden, before we were driven to church in a vintage car, decorated especially for the day.

When we arrived at the church I looked down the aisle and spotted John standing at the front, waiting for me. I wanted to run – I couldn't wait to be standing next to him. As the organ played the notes of the first hymn, I took my dad's arm, proud that he was looking so healthy and sober, and smart in his top hat and tails. As we walked down the aisle, him holding tightly onto my hand, I looked around the church at all the people who'd played such a huge part in my life. Ryan and Ellen sat over on one side, and Anne and Jayne sat together near the front in pride of place behind my family. Clare was there with her husband and new baby girl, and I knew that Sam would be thinking of me in Paraguay even though she couldn't be there. Caroline was standing behind a microphone ready to sing, but already wiping away tears. As I reached the front I caught sight of Mum and David, both crying as they saw how happy I was.

I only just managed to contain the tears as I said my vows. As I promised to be with John for the rest of my life it struck me how much love, care and hard work had gone into me living to see this day. As we sat in the front row, newly married, I realized again how fortunate I was to have so many dear friends. I listened to Michelle's husband Andy read the Bible, prayed with Allison as she prayed for us, and wept as Caroline sang about Jesus being the rock upon which we build our lives. I had never felt so blessed.

The reception was gorgeous. My mother-in-law had decorated the room with miles of hanging white muslin, and I was surrounded by white roses. I ate what I wanted, drank what I wanted, and relished every second of giving a speech and handing out thank-you presents. As we cut the cake that Anne had made for us, I turned to smile at her. I had spent many hours in her kitchen watching her make cakes for everyone she knew, but I'd never eaten a crumb. She understood and winked at me, and I chuckled.

"What are you giggling at?" John whispered in my ear.

"Nothing, darling," I smiled. He would never know the me who panicked at the mere sight of cake.

As the lights dimmed and the music started, my husband held out his hand for our first dance.

"This is the happiest I've ever been," I whispered into his lapel. "Thank you, Lord."

Epilogue

I wish I could give you a final equation, the one thing that pulled me out of the self-destructive cycle for good. But I can't. Recovery is a long road that still stretches out of sight. I no longer self-harm, but I'm still growing up. The difference is that the road is a scenic one, so I'm able to keep going and enjoy the view. I can't even say that it's all fun, but I want to take each day as it comes, to see what's around the next corner, to learn from the people I meet on the journey.

There was no clanging bell, no charismatic healing service, no loud and raucous praying, and no being slain in the spirit. There was just a tiny switch in my head, as if God just said, "Hmmm, I think now is the time." And I realized that what I was living was not what life is all about.

Don't get me wrong – it had nothing to do with me and everything to do with God. He was the one who came along and broke in – first when I was seventeen and became a Christian, and then numerous times in subsequent years as I chose to give my struggles, doubts, fears and bad choices up to him. Perhaps my biggest mistake was thinking that he would do it all for me, that he would swoop down and heal me and I would be a prime example of a miraculous healing of biblical proportions. In some ways I would love to be able to tell that story, and I have been angry at God many times for not making it happen. It would have been such a small job for him, and so much easier for me. But I have learned so much through striving for recovery that I wouldn't change my story. My struggle towards wholeness has made me who I am. It is difficult now, as I look back and see his plan coming together in a way I neither expected nor desired, to admit how much I doubted God.

Through all those years of struggling, when I wasn't being miraculously healed, I would yell at God in private, while proclaiming in public that God's plan was best. It wasn't that I didn't believe that God's plan was better, but I was so caught up in my own pain that I couldn't see how his plan was ever going to work. And as it turns out, of course, my public proclamation was the more accurate. It is a powerful and humbling experience to look back and see the threads of God's hope and love worked intricately into the tapestry of my past, even at those darkest times when I felt I was all alone in the world and about to give up.

God is a healing God – but he doesn't always heal in the way we want him to. He sets people free, but we don't always look hard enough to see it. He set me free in a miraculous way by dying on the cross – I am free from the consequences of all my straying because of that one divine, mystical event that I still don't fully understand, and never will this side of eternity. Early on in my walk of faith, that miracle had the power to hold me in awe and wonder, and there have been points of clarity since where I have recognized again the wonder of the cross. But all Christians can be guilty of forgetting – we forget what it was like not to be imbued with the word of God, we forget the passion we once had, and we forget what it was like to be lost. Then we start to think that God is unfair. We forget that he gave up his Son for us, and we start to complain that he hasn't healed us, or that he hasn't made things happen the way we want them to, or that he seems distant. Even after the long story I've just told, I'm still guilty of this. I still resist God's plan when it's not my own, and I still complain when he doesn't answer my prayers in the way I think is best. Fortunately, God is loving and full of grace and puts up with my whining and continues to teach me how to be his child.

With 20/20 hindsight I can see much more clearly the lessons that God quietly slipped into the midst of the dark times. Through my time at Kainos he showed me that I had the means to get myself better, and that I had resources I'd not tapped into yet. God showed me that he had created me with strength, that I was a person worth saving, and that I had an ability to fight. He taught me that I could rely on those inner strengths, and that I had more within myself than I thought. Later, he taught me that I could rely on him, that he had strength I would never understand. He showed me that he would never let me go and that I would never be alone. And God used my last time of struggle to teach me about fellowship – I learned that I could allow other people to support me and lean on friends in times of need. I learned that I didn't have to do everything alone because God had given me strength through my friends, who are my brothers and sisters in Christ. In trying to be the perfect Christian I had never let them support me. I had to let my defenses down and trust other people more.

I have also learned that Christians are just as capable of being in pain as anyone else. I had naively imagined that all Christians spent their private lives behind closed doors singing praises and raising their hands to the Lord, and that I was the only one doing things like sticking my fingers down my throat, cutting my own flesh and cooking wholesome meals out of a tub of cottage cheese and a bag of frozen spinach. But Christians do struggle with pain – the public times of bereavement and loss, but also the private pains of addictions, depression, childlessness, sexuality, debt. We just don't like to talk about it. We don't like to admit that we struggle with the biblical promises of not being given more than we can bear and God being in control. But I don't want to deny any of that. It is for freedom that Christ has set me free, and I intend to live in that freedom, enjoy it, shout about it from the rooftops. My story is a testimony to the power of God, his strength in my weakness and his amazing gift to us.

So, life changed. I worked hard. I went to counselling, and I cried my way through tissues and friends. I didn't come out of it unscathed – I carry the memories around on my body. I can never leave that part of my life completely behind, because I see reminders of it every day. People question me or, worse, talk to my scars rather than my face and don't ask questions. I hate to say it, but the latter are often the Christians who don't want to risk asking in case I might tell them what it was like to be so far from God that I wanted to end it all and give up on ever seeing his glory.

But the scars are good, too. They remind me that I survived. They remind me that I am strong enough to survive in the future. They remind me that God has grace – enough to go around and then some. They show my weakness, which means that they daily show me the power he has to hold me up.

Someone once saw the scars on my arm and, knowing a little of my history, said, "You were a silly girl, weren't you."

I didn't have the courage then to rise above it, and I regretfully smiled and moved the conversation on. I wish I had been brave enough to say, "No, I wasn't silly, I was a survivor."

Despite everything, against all the odds, I am still here. And, more than that, I am happy. I love life. I love people and the sky and chocolate cake and rabbits and pianos, and I love my God. I'm still here.

Finding Help

Adullam Ministries

Adullam is the organization that grew out of Abbie's work with self-harmers. Our main emphasis is on raising awareness of self-harm within the church, and we run workshops for anyone who wants to understand self-harm, whether sufferers or carers. We also offer training for counsellors and other professionals (nurses, teachers, prison staff and others), providing a deeper understanding of self-harm and offering mechanisms for use with self-harming clients.

Our website includes information both on self-harm and on the Christian faith. It features safe alternatives, survivors' stories and moderated forums, whereby sufferers can share their struggles in a safe and anonymous environment.

Our contact details are as follows:

Adullam Ministries
P.O. Box 4101
Rugby
Warwickshire
UK, CV21 9BF
Phone: 00 (44) 7743 525931
www.adullam-ministries.org.uk
Email: adullam@adullam-ministries.org.uk

Kainos Trust

In 2004, Kainos Trust merged with another charity, Nicholaston House (part of Swansea City Mission), which is based in Gower, Swansea. However, Helena still offers support to those affected by eating disorders, mainly through residential courses.

Contact details:

Nicholaston House
Penmaen Gower
Swansea
Wales, SA3 2HL
Phone: 00 (44) 1792 371317
www.nicholastonhouse.org
Email: managers@nicholastonhouse.org

Self-harm

The Amber Project, based in Cardiff, offers all levels of support to young people who self-harm. Although their services are aimed specifically at those living in Cardiff, they publish various resources for sixteen to twenty-five year olds, which can be purchased through their office.

Contact details:

The Amber Project
Room One
The Quaker Meeting House
43 Charles Street
Cardiff
Wales CF10 2HB
Phone: 00 (44) 29 20344776
www.tybronna.org.uk/Amber%20project.htm
Email: staff@tybronna.fslife.co.uk

Bristol Crisis Service for Women is a national voluntary organization, again based in the U.K., that supports women in emotional distress, particularly those who self-harm. They have a national helpline available for anyone to talk for up to an hour, with a translator if necessary: 00 (44) 117 925 1119. Their address on the web is
www.users.zetnet.co.uk/bcsw

Zest (Northern Ireland) offers a one-to-one counselling program, which often involves other family members too. The project manager (and young person's counsellor) is based in Derry. The outreach counsellor has weekly clinics in Enniskillen, Coleraine and Belfast. Telephone-based support is also available if you cannot easily travel to one of their four locations. They also offer some training events.
Phone: 00 (44) 28 7126 6999
www.zestni.org
Email: zestni@yahoo.co.uk

S.A.F.E. Alternatives (Self-Abuse Finally Ends) is a recognized treatment approach, professional network and educational resource base operating in the U.S. and Canada. S.A.F.E. is committed to helping people achieve an end to self-injurious behavior.
S.A.F.E. Alternatives
10 Bergman Ct.
Forest Park, IL 60130
USA
Phone: 1-800-DONTCUT or 708-366-9066
www.selfinjury.com

Eating disorders

ABC is a Christian organization in the UK run by Christians for sufferers and their families and carers. They offer resources, advice, support and a chance to share experiences with others who have dealt with similar issues.

Contact details:

ABC
PO Box 173
Letchworth
Hertfordshire
UK, SG6 1XQ
www.anorexiabulimiacare.co.uk

The National Eating Disorders Association (NEDA) is the largest not-for-profit organization in the United States working to prevent eating disorders and provide treatment referrals to those suffering from anorexia, bulimia and binge eating disorders and those concerned with body image and weight issues.

www.edap.org

The Eating Disorders Foundation of Victoria is a nonprofit organization in Australia which aims to support those affected by eating disorders, and to better inform the community about disordered eating.

1513 High Street
Glen Iris
VIC 3146
Australia
Phone: 03 9885 0318
www.eatingdisorders.org.au
Email: edfv@eatingdisorders.org.au

Related issues

It is estimated that around 50% of people who self-harm have also been sexually abused. Life Centre is based on the south coast of England and offers counselling and support for people who've been through any kind of sexual violation.

Contact details:

**Life Centre
P.O. Box 58
Chichester
West Sussex
UK, PO19 8UD
www.lifecentre.uk.com
Email: info@lifecentre.uk.com**

Life Centre also runs a helpline which is open on Thursdays and Sundays from 7.30 – 10 p.m. G.M.T.: 00 00 (44) 1243 779196.

Mercy Ministries

Mercy Ministries is a non-profit organization that exists to assist and meet the needs of young women who face life-controlling problems such as drug and alcohol abuse, addictions, depression, self-harm, eating disorders and unplanned pregnancy. They provide a free residential treatment program designed to address the whole person: spiritual, physical and emotional. Founded in America, they now have centers in America, Australia, and England and are exploring the possibilities of additional centers in New Zealand, Canada and Peru.

Mercy Ministries of America
Corporate Office
P.O. Box 111060
Nashville, TN 37222-1060
USA
Phone: 615-831-6987
www.mercyministries.com
Email: info@mercyministries.com

Mercy Ministries Canada
6788 152 Street
Surrey, BC
V3S 3L4
Phone: 604-596-2422
www.mercycanada.com
Email: admin@mercycanada.com

Mercy Ministries Australia
P.O. Box 1537
Castle Hill
NSW
1765
Australia
Phone: +61 2 9659 4180 or 1 800 011 537
www.mercyministries.com.au
Email: info@mercyministries.com.au

Mercy Ministries UK
Cragg Royd
Lowertown
Oxenhope
BD22 9JE, UK
Phone: 00 (44) 1535 642 042
www.mercyministries.co.uk
Email: info@mercyministries.co.uk

Some useful websites

www.selfharm.org.uk
www.siari.co.uk
www.something-fishy.org/
www.mirror-mirror.org/eatdis.htm

Acknowledgements

Very big and real thanks go to . . .

My family, for always being there and digging me out of holes. Mum, for being so amazing in helping me write and for remembering things you'd rather forget – you are a superstar. The in-laws, for being so supportive and telling me to follow my calling. Jayne and Graham – you're as close to family as it's possible to be.

The bodies of Christ at Enfield Baptist and Bilton Evangelical churches, who made me one of their own and encouraged me to grow. And the friends I've made over the years – too many to mention, but some I have to name: Lucy, for never giving up; Helena and Nikki, for teaching me so much and making me feel useful; Michelle, for 1 a.m. life plans and telling me I can achieve things; Allison, for the not-quite conversations that punctuated our exhaustion; Andrew, for being a true friend when it mattered; and Sam – you are never as far away as you feel. You have been so much help, my life is richer with you in it.

Caroline, my fellow word lover, for always telling me the truth, even if what I've written is utter pants. Corinne and Clare, for your expert opinions when I wanted to throw it away and for encouragement when I thought I was never going to get it finished.

Ali Hull, for always believing in this project, even when I wasn't so sure. This book would not be half the book it is without your genius and refreshing bluntness. Nick Page, for finding me a title and teaching me so much about writing. Tara Smith, editor extraordinaire, for being so amazingly kind and gentle. Charlotte and the team at Authentic, who put this together and made it a real live book.

Anne, for telling me to write in the first place, and for constantly encouraging me not to give up on life, even when it got hard. You always believed there was more in me than self-destruction. You play such a big part in this story. You are an angel.

My John, for whom no adjective is enough. Thank you for sorting out my laptop and my life, for putting up with my working at midnight and consequent grumpiness, for teaching me what love is and isn't, and for wanting me despite everything. I love you.

And to the Lord my God. You are the one who wrote my story – I am just adding the words and hoping I can do justice to your creativity. I owe this story, and my life, to you.